INVOCATIONS

Invocations

The Poetry and Prose
of Gwendolyn MacEwen

Jan Bartley

UNIVERSITY OF BRITISH COLUMBIA PRESS

Vancouver

INVOCATIONS
The Poetry and Prose
of Gwendolyn MacEwen

© The University of British Columbia 1983

This book has been published with the help of a grant from the
Canadian Federation for the Humanities, using funds provided by the
Social Sciences and Humanities Research Council of Canada.

Canadian Cataloguing in Publication Data

Bartley, Jan.
Invocations

Includes index.
Bibliography: p.
ISBN 0-7748-0177-8

1. MacEwen, Gwendolyn, 1941–   – Criticism
and interpretation. I. Title.
PS8525.E92Z56   C811'.54   C83-091187-1
PR9199.3.M323Z56

International Standard Book Number 0-7748-0177-8
Printed in Canada

Contents

List of Abbreviations

AM	*The Armies of the Moon*
BB	*A Breakfast for Barbarians*
FE	*The Fire-Eaters*
JM	*Julian the Magician*
KE,KD	*King of Egypt, King of Dreams*
MA	*Magic Animals*
N	*Noman*
RF	*The Rising Fire*
SM	*The Shadow-Maker*
TW	*The Trojan Women*

Preface

If it is permissible or even possible to apply a single adjective to the aim of Gwendolyn MacEwen's writing, then the most accurate word would be explorative. All of her publications to date have been concerned with a quest for a particular knowledge or vision and, consequently, with the communication of such knowledge to her audience. Ordinarily, this would not appear to be an onerous task for so gifted an artist; but the repeatedly mystic nature of MacEwen's vision demands from her a much more complex process of communication than that which can be achieved through language alone. In order to grasp the intangible "mystery, joy, and passion of life"[1] which she strives to reveal—in order to appreciate the prophet as much as the poet—statements of emotion, dogma, and personal theory are insufficient. It is not surprising therefore, that MacEwen has provided her readers with many signposts which, if heeded, will help to guide them into her "fifth earth," the birthplace of "Orbiting castles and giants and starbeasts"[2] of myth, ambiguity, personal terror, and ecstasy. Through a combination of concrete detail and application of "kinetic mythology," that is, "myth alive and re-enacted in the spontaneous actions of real people,"[3] she is able to blend the human and divine, thereby transmuting ordinary phenomena into arcane revelation. The purpose of this book is to heed the author's signposts, to examine the numerous sources and influences which are indicated by the epigrams and symbols included in her writing. An investigation of such references will provide a key to the imagery of MacEwen's prose and poetry and enable the reader to participate more fully in her perceptual and spiritual explorations.

At this point it is necessary to stress that however helpful the links may be between background material and MacEwen's publications, the major emphasis will be placed on the latter. The sources which I plan to deal with should be regarded chiefly as springboards into a more intelligent discussion of the merits and flaws of MacEwen's prose and poetry. At no time should they be considered of overriding importance, or as subjects of concern worthy of discussion that is independent of their relationship to and influence upon MacEwen's writing. The logic of such an approach is based on MacEwen's own declaration that many of the parallels to psychology and myth which seem so striking are, in fact, purely accidental.[4] Thus it would seem foolish to discuss the validity and particular interests of the sources in themselves at the expense of MacEwen's creative results. Background material and other influences upon the author act as catalysts to creativity; thus, in the process of unravelling MacEwen's poetic adventures, they can best be considered as catalysts to discovery.

Much of the symbolism and imagery used by MacEwen has its origin in myth, religion, philosophy, psychology, and historical tradition. While it is my intention to enhance the effectiveness of such incorporated imagery by linking its active function in the prose and poetry to its original meaning, it would be impossible to isolate and discuss every symbol in such a manner. Most of my attention will be directed towards major patterns of symbolism, which include the imagery of light and dark, gold and silver, the revolving wheel or circle, the rising fire, the magician figure, and the dancer. Perhaps the most significant and certainly the two most fascinating figures are the mystic and the multi-faceted Muse. The frustrations of the mystic quest are a major theme of MacEwen's prose, while the amorphous presence of a masculine Muse is the dominant symbol of her poetry. By noting their implications, variations, and degrees of effectiveness, it may be possible to trace not only the poet's meanings but also any indications of development in her style.

Although an examination of form and style is not a central consideration of this book, there is a notable improvement from MacEwen's earlier writing to her most recent. Her application of myth and background material reflects a growing assurance and command of poetic techniques and prose style. However, it is difficult to isolate stages of development in her writing, since much of the prose and poetry was written simultaneously and not necessarily in the order of specific publication. Nevertheless, the most sensible way to facilitate a recognition of development seems to be by adhering to the chronology of publication. I suspect it would be difficult for Mac-Ewen to remember exactly when each piece of fiction or each collection of poems was written or to supply any more exact order. Although it may be simpler to discuss the prose first and the poetry later, I feel that a chronological arrangement will not only assist in the observation of MacEwen's maturing process but will also serve to demonstrate the many similarities of theme and imagery between selected samples of her writing. Throughout her work, certain motifs and characters are presented in both prosaic and poetic form. There is a definite complementary effect when such pieces are considered together. The ability of MacEwen to work with confidence in two media without seeming repetitious is an achievement which should not be ignored.

In conclusion, it should be noted that the lack of criticism concerning Gwendolyn MacEwen has prompted the large scope of this book. Of the material that is available most articles are little more than superficial reviews, with the exception of five publications which attempt to consider some aspect of her writing in detail. Since it is my basic assumption that Gwendolyn MacEwen is a unique and established artist, my intention is to remedy this lack and to initiate further discussion of her talents. Certainly no one study can deal inclusively with her variety of range and mood or with the richness of her vision. Thus, it should be considered, like MacEwen's work itself, as an exploration rather than as a final statement.

I am grateful to Frank Davey, Gwendolyn MacEwen, Jack David and Michael Rehner, all of whom have given generously of their time, patience and expertise in the writing of this book. Thanks are also due to Heather Campbell, Ron Kiverago, Joan Smith, Shirley Temple and Secretarial Services at York University, for assistance at various stages in preparing the manuscript.

J.L. Bartley
York University

1

The Discovery

do not imagine that the exploration
ends, that she has yielded all her mystery
or that the map you hold
cancels further discovery

I tell you her uncovering takes years,
takes centuries, and when you find her naked
look again,
admit there is something else you cannot name,
a veil, a coating just above the flesh
which you cannot remove by your mere wish

when you see the land naked, look again
(burn your maps, that is not what I mean),
I mean the moment when it seems most plain
is the moment when you must begin again

The circular pattern of "The Discovery," a poem published in *The Shadow-Maker* (1969), is an indication of the pattern of exploration necessary in the 'uncovering' of Gwendolyn MacEwen's writing—an uncovering that does yield mystery but which also eludes final statements. MacEwen's elusiveness, her evocation of the marvellous amid the mundane, and her celebrations of an "improvised eden" amid a fragmented cosmos, provide both a distinctive voice in Canadian literature, and an aura of impenetrability that fascinates but also baffles her audience.

Born in 1941 in Toronto, MacEwen emerged from the 1960's, a period frequently referred to as a Canadian renaissance in poetry. After she left school at eighteen, she wrote three unpublished novels. One of these later became the short story, "Day of Twelve Princes." MacEwen was not then, nor is she now, aligned with any group of poets—the courage to begin was an individual one. "I can't trace where the original impulse came from but I always wanted to write."[1] As Geddes suggests, her motivation was combined with confidence:

> Aestheticians might say that a preoccupation with process reflects only the necessary understanding that in art there is nothing to be said only ways of saying it. Gwendolyn MacEwen is not of this persuasion. For a young poet, she writes with surprising confidence in her own capacities and in the authenticity of her undertaking. She rejects self-indulgent, therapeutic poetry and the 'terribly cynical and "cool" poetry written today.' She believes that the poet can and must say things; and she writes with the conviction that she has discovered things sayable, and worth saying. 'I write basically to communicate joy, mystery, passion,' she says, '... not the joy that naively exists without knowledge of pain, but that joy which arises out of and conquers pain. I want to construct a myth.'[2]

The shaping of MacEwen's myth has sustained a prolific career: two pamphlets, *The Drunken Clock* and *Selah* (1961); *Julian the Magician* (1963); *The Rising Fire* (1963); *A Breakfast for Barbarians* (1966); *The Shadow-Maker* (1969); *King of Egypt, King of Dreams* (1971); *Armies of the Moon* (1972); *Noman* (1972); *Magic Animals* (1974); *The Fire-Eaters* (1976); *Mermaids and Ikons: A Greek Summer* (1978); *The T.E. Lawrence Poems* (1982); and *Earthlight* (Selected Poems) 1963–1982 (1982). In addition she has written several CBC radio plays and documentary programmes. One verse play *Terror and Erebus* was published in *Tamarack* (1974). MacEwen's adaptation of Euripides' *The Trojan Women* was performed at the St. Lawrence Centre in Toronto in 1978 and published, together with the Greek poetry of Yannis Ritsos in 1981. She has also published two books for juveniles: *The Chocolate Moose* (1979) and *The Honey Drum* (1983). Currently she is completing a new novel, "which begins on the other side of the archway in *Noman*."[3] MacEwen's experience with the theatre, afforded by the production of *The Trojan Women*, was so personally rewarding in a creative sense that she plans to write more plays: "If this country has any legitimate theme, it's that of the immigrant, and I am writing a modern play about the Greek immigrants in the Danforth area.[4]

MacEwen has a clear sense of her own development, although she was not aware of certain recurring themes, such as the Muse, until Margaret Atwood drew her attention to it. She also confesses some measure of embarrassment over the unevenness of her early writing: "I was very young," she says, "and the work reflects that. The novel [*Julian*] especially is technically flawed."[5]

MacEwen does not want to see a reprinted edition of her first novel, *Julian the Magician*, written when she was nineteen and published when she was only twenty-two, and in *Magic Animals*, which includes a section of selected poems, she has included only fourteen from *Selah*, *The Drunken Clock*, and *The Rising Fire* combined. Now, after slightly more than twenty years of writing (at age seventeen, her first poems appeared in *The Canadian Forum*) she is remarkably secure and honest about her career, a career clearly stamped by an early statement of intent: "I am involved with writing as a total profession, not as an aesthetic pursuit.... My prime concern has always been with the raw materials from which literature is derived, not with literature as an end in itself."[6]

MacEwen's raw materials embrace a wide range of esoteric and psychological sources—Jacob Boehme, the early Christian gnostic texts, Jung, and, most notably, alchemy, the ancient art of transmuting metal, personalities, and antithetical properties into a unified and transcending whole known as *coniunctio oppositorum*, the marriage of opposites. The key to the interrelationship among MacEwen's sources is her emphasis on internal explorations, on self-examination. She focuses on the Gnostic values of internal salvation, on Jungian principles of self-discovery, and on the psychological interpretations of alchemy, in which the actual physical materials used by the alchemist become projections of an individual unconscious. Thus, the chemical process of alchemy, the transmutation of lead into gold, becomes a metaphor of a spiritual process, a quest for inner vision and totality. The quest for totality becomes possible when opposites are reconciled. Accordingly, throughout her writing, MacEwen stresses the dualistic philosophy of the hermetic tradition: she employs the dualities of mind/body, spirit/matter, and their application, in the area of psychology, to the conscious and unconscious realms of man's psyche. She makes frequent reference to the destruction-creation, stasis-movement processes of alchemy, and to Boehme's philosophy that "the opposition of all essences is basic."[7] Most significantly, MacEwen explores the very sensual and unholy mixtures of what Frank Davey calls our "Heraclitean" world. If she draws her sense of myth and mystery in part from her source material, she perceives it as being unmistakably alive in the sensual world, and through an increasing use of concrete imagery, translates her vision into a recognizably post-modernist sensibility.

MacEwen's vision and complex language embrace both the traditionally poetic and modern colloquial. In Canadian literature, she bridges the gap between the poets who rely heavily on myth, such as James Reaney and Jay MacPherson, and the more experimental poets of her own generation such as George Bowering and Michael Ondaatje. But even though her roots are well known and her position in Canadian literature well established, Mac-Ewen is often seen as outside, or at least on the periphery of, the mainstream of the Canadian poetic imagination.

This departure from the mainstream prompts both praise and uneasiness. In an early review of *Julian the Magician*, Elizabeth Barrett rejoices over the disappearance of the stock Cabbagetown setting and the "Baffinland vignettes":

> To my knowledge, this is one of the first novels by Canadian authors that has none of the ingenue's introversion or the patriot's zeal: in short, it is one of the few pieces of good fiction to come out of Canada not plainly stamped Canadian.[8]

In a similar vein, John Robert Colombo, in *How Do I Love Thee*, refers to *Julian the Magician* and *The Twelve Circles of the Night* (an early title for *King of Egypt, King of Dreams*) as "mystic."[9] The anthologizer Gary Geddes adds: "MacEwen's poetry might well be discussed in terms of the peculiar ground it inhabits between the 'realists' and the 'myth-makers' in Canadian poetry. From the beginning she has repudiated the actual world for one that is ancient and mythic."[10]

MacEwen's "peculiar ground" is one sketched out by language as well as thematic concern. In an early review of *The Rising Fire*, Bowering focuses on her distinctiveness:

> The language of the poems is a language of ambition, of wanting. It stands outside the mainstream of current Canadian poetry, which seems generally to belong to the post-Williams age. That is, Miss MacEwen's language is the opposite to the language of (our purest example) Raymond Souster. One is aware of something like poetic diction, not the rhythmic arrangement of a prose line. In a poem like "All the Fine Young Horses," for instance, her "issues" if she claims any, are not of matter and the senses, but of a young feminine, *personal* imagination. Anthology-makers or those who teach survey courses might call her a Romantic.[11]

The danger of distinctiveness is, of course, incomprehension—a point to which Bowering alludes when he writes, "Miss MacEwen's usual unwillingness to be direct sets a distance at first. She is not an immediate poet in this time of immediacy."[12] In a much later review of *The Armies of the Moon*, Michael Hornyansky echoes this warning, albeit in a more ironic way: "Even in homier dimensions her manner remains highly characteristic, or 'different' as we say in Canada."[13]

Indeed, MacEwen's esoteric and metaphorical journeys into Greece and Egypt, outer and inner space, the landscape of "The Fifth Earth" with its "purple castles," "demons," and "dark stars" are often perceived to be private journeys—journeys in which the reader may be a spectator, even a marvelling spectator, but not a participant. The major limitation on MacEwen's prose and poetry, which emerges from a survey of the available criticism, is that her vision is, at times, an obscure one. When language, emotion, and experience combine, her poems are startling—convincing almost in the manner of a personal revelation. When she slips into excessive theorizing or ecstatic diction, her poems are either too obvious or too hazy, like whispered secrets one cannot quite hear. Thus, Dave Godfrey complains, in a review of *Julian the Magician*, that "the Myth Renovators should acknowledge at least one law: the greater and more familiar the myth, the greater the effort needed before renovation is successful."[14] His general opinion of the novel is that MacEwen "has dreamed up more than she can mysticate." Similarly, Frank Davey, in "Gwendolyn MacEwen: The Secret of Alchemy," points to poems "which...read like mysteriously excerpted dialogue from a hidden play," and rejoices in the concreteness of *A Breakfast for Barbarians*: "Gone is the inflated poetic language of the first two books [*Julian the Magician* and *The Rising Fire*] which presented MacEwen as a variation of the ecstatic dryad."[15]

Although MacEwen's failure to communicate the unspeakable is largely confined to her early publications, some critics see her vision and her language as persistently extravagant and shadowy. Yet, these same critics find much to praise in MacEwen. For example, Milton Wilson speaks of a "wide-ranging, half-disciplined imagination;"[16] Eli Mandel of "atrocious puns, execrable metaphors, impossible analogies....a language which 'explodes, for instance.'"[17] The majority of criticism which deals with *A Breakfast for Barbarians* and with works published afterwards is positive, but qualified by comments which continue to point to excess in language and exclusiveness of concern. Kathy Mezei, in a favourable review of *Noman*, adds that the author "sometimes oversteps the line between fantasy and obscurity, between excursions into another reality and excursions into a writer's private and exclusive world."[18]

The Shadow-Maker, which won the Governor-General's Award for poetry in 1969, caused mixed reactions. These are best articulated by Gail Fox, who praises the "gentle recklessness" of MacEwen's poetry, "a desire to take risks and bear the consequences," but who also regrets a "less daring, more subdued and almost conventional and commonplace" note in the imagery.[19] Fox's impression, echoed by Davey in his review, stems from a shift in tone between the "vigorous actuality" of *A Breakfast* and the more introspective and sometimes deliberately fantastic mood of *The Shadow-Maker*. Fox points to figures of speech which are "embarrassing" and "futile" and ends her review on a note which is half-disappointed, half-hopeful:

> Poems I object to in *The Shadow-Maker* are ones such as "Dream Three: The Child" which ends with this line: "and I looked and I saw it was me." This genre of ending is like that of the novel whose author gets tired of the main protagonist, and has him killed off somehow on the last page. Very easy, and what a let-down!... "The beast is taming," she writes in another disappointing poem, "The Taming of the Dragon." Perhaps the poet is also taming. But I would prefer to think this about her new poetry: "it is not lost, it is moving forward always."[20]

Clearly then, a lack of discipline and control emerges as the single most persistent flaw in MacEwen's writing. If her urgency to communicate myth is not tempered by patience, not made accessible through dramatic situation, then, poetically, the result may be manipulated rhymes and dogmatic statement, or the excesses of private reverie.

Nevertheless, MacEwen's exuberance is, of itself, attractive, and perhaps this explains why, almost unanimously, unfavourable criticisms of her writing begin to sound like praise or, at the very least, are qualified by a sense of admiration. Many of MacEwen's critics are themselves poets, and although this is not at all unusual in Canadian literature, it is a fact which perhaps further explains why the exuberance which tends to flaw her vision also fascinates. Davey, Bowering, Fox, D.G. Jones, Ralph Gustafson, and Mandel are themselves not immune to the energy of poetic utterance, however unsuccessful its thematic or semantic content. Thus, Bowering writes:

> Gwendolyn MacEwen gives eloquent testimony to the fact that artificial imagery can still be expressed with beautifully chosen sound patterns, and that is what makes her poetry worthwhile. Her very deliberate sound values, the choosing of syllables, result from an impulse to make up for discarded end rhyme... the images are young and feminine and surrealistic... Miss MacEwen's [poetry] strikes as competent "scored" music. Unfortunately, it is often difficult to make out what she is singing about.[21]

Similarly, Mandel labels her vibrant phrasing as "the very stuff of creation";[22] Milton Wilson speaks of her early poems as being not so much finished as a "fluent scatter of evocative phrases," poems which fail "originally."[23] Fox refers to MacEwen as a rare poet whose rhythm and sonorous patterns of speech surround one "with the feeling that a spell has been cast and that one is in the middle of this spell."[24] Finally, Gustafson offers this review, which perceptively identifies the vice of MacEwen's early poetry as being also one of her major themes:

> Mostly these days, Pegasus pulls a hack. But not always. Way back in 1963...Gwendolyn MacEwen wrote that as the horizons of the world widened for her, "the poetry moved parallel, shifting, forming new complexities and sudden simplicities." Mostly her work is "to chalk out quickly the peril of beauty." As her work has progressed, however, there has appeared a dangerous tendency to devote everything to inward complexity; to confine repetitive communication to the demon of her darker self, the red beast who moves her blood where there is civil war. The pursuit is carried even into an elegy on someone else. Her poetry, at those times, is as egocentric as a dream.
>
> That MacEwen is aware of this danger is proved (and proved beautifully) by her novel *King of Egypt, King of Dreams*. The theme of the novel is of the wreckage which a dream imposes.[25]

With few exceptions (Don Precosky offers an uncompromisingly negative review of *The Fire-Eaters*; E.R. Zietlow dismisses *Noman*), even the criticism of MacEwen is reminiscent of the circular structure of "The Discovery." The "uncovering" which occasionally yields too impenetrable a mystery creates also a fascination in that the mystery itself informs a distinctive poetic vision. This double-edged quality is given its most explicit claim in this review by Joseph Sherman:

> I am not at all sure why it is that I like and admire her poetry. Perhaps because she is so magnificently obscure, and that has always invited something like admiration. She casts such a thick and strangely woven cloth over her work that it is, at the best of times, translucent. But so skillful is she in her poetic craft that the reader is attracted again and again to her work, partly because so little can be fathomed at first reading, and partly because what is, at one moment, clear, shifts in the next moment to a further extension of meaning, or even to new meaning.[26]

As Gustafson, Davey, and Atwood state explicitly, the task of transmuting the ordinary into the ethereal, of making the word flesh, the arcane incarnate, is MacEwen's primary task and the central theme in her prose and poetry. Throughout the corpus of MacEwen's writing, the unifying perception is one which seeks to uncover the mythological in the mundane. Accordingly, her version of *The Trojan Women* explores the first and final "enemy": the self. Even *Mermaids and Ikons*, a travel book "written for fun," begins with a woman who fancies herself "as a kind of Zeus giving birth to Athena from [her] split skull." Of her early statement "I want to create a myth" Mac-Ewen says, "I used to use that phrase as a kind of quotable quote, but I'm not sure if it's quite accurate. It's not so much a matter of invention as of perception—in a way it's more a matter of saying what I see."[27] It is important to realize that MacEwen is not refuting the validity of the myth but stressing her personal involvement in a complex world in which the myth is inherent, and renewed, and reinterpreted in the process of day-to-day living. An earlier comment makes the poet's position clear:

> In my poetry I am concerned with finding the relationships between what we call the "real" world and that other world which consists of dream, fantasy and myth. I've never felt that these "two worlds" are as separate as one might think, and in fact my poetry as well as my life seems to occupy a place—you might call it a kind of no-man's land— between the two. Very often experiences or observations which are immediate take on grand or universal significance for me, because they seem to capsulize and give new force to the age-old wonders, mysteries and fears which have always delighted and bewildered mankind. In my attempt to describe a world which is for me both miraculous and ter-rible, I make abundant use of myth, metaphor and symbol; these are as much a part of my language as the alphabet I use.[28]

MacEwen, then, has incorporated myth, in both a personal and an artistic sense. It defines the boundaries of her perception and informs her explorations of inner and outer space. It is translated verbally through paradox, inverse logic, the juxtaposition of the profound and the profane, and a mixed diction of symbolic and colloquial speech. Above all, the myth is neither a literary device nor the formalistic system of a modernist, but the totally involved searchings of a post-modernist amid a cataclysmic environment.

Insight into the more particular features of MacEwen's myth is afforded by Atwood, Davey, and Ellen D. Warwick, each of whom has attempted to deal with the poet's language, imagery, and thematic concern in some detail. For Atwood, the dominant figure of MacEwen's poetry is the male "Muse," the unnamed "you" of the poems whose amorphous presence allows, for both poet and reader, the possibility of comprehending a holy universe in the midst of a burgeoning disorder:

> MacEwen is not a poet interested in turning her life into myth; rather she is concerned with translating her myth into life, and into the poetry

which is a part of it. The informing Myth... is that of the Muse, author and inspirer of language and therefore of the ordered verbal cosmos, the poet's universe.... He is a dancer and a singer; his dance and his song are the Word made flesh, and both contain and create order and reality.... The Muse is both "good" and "evil," both gentle and violent, both creative and destructive; like language itself, he subsumes all opposites. Since he is infinite, the number of his incarnations is potentially infinite also.[29]

The most compelling aspect of the Muse is his dynamism—he is never stagnant but continually assuming new shapes, never totally revealed before dancing into new forms, fresh landscapes. He may appear as pure imagination in the realm of dream and fantasy or as a creature half-divine, half-human, incarnate as king, magician, athlete, dancer, singer, or lover.

Furthermore, since the Muse, master of disguise and revelation, subsumes all opposites, he is reminiscent of the winged god Mercurius who presides over the process of alchemy, a process which strives for the synthesizing *coniunctio oppositorum*, the marriage of opposites. MacEwen's writing abounds with alchemical imagery, and her structures mirror the cyclical creation and destruction of the alchemical process. The Jungian influence in MacEwen's prose and poetry suggests yet another source for the Muse—that of an animus figure who, through his various postures, may reveal something of the nature of the total self—a harmonious potential innate in the individual.

In the article "Gwendolyn MacEwen: The Secret of Alchemy," Davey elaborates on the myth by stating that the lesson of the alchemists, "that the divine is attained only through its union with the material—through the blending of light and dark, good and evil, sun and moon,"[30] necessitates a dualistic vision. MacEwen's task is to reveal that vision in her prose and poetry, a task that is realized only when the alchemical lesson is self-absorbed: that is, when she seeks "the flesh of situation to give the ideas of her poetry living artistic form."[31] MacEwen, in her own art, seeks to achieve the miracle of transubstantiation in which the mythic is made flesh. It is this achievement which Davey uses to distinguish between the ornamental and kinetic application of myth.

The most outstanding technical feature of these novels and stories [Davey is reviewing *Julian, King of Egypt, King of Dreams*, and *Noman*] is that the various myths seldom appear merely superimposed on the action. The leading characters—Akhenaton, It Neter Ay, Julian, Noman, Kali—are all convincingly drawn figures, with plausible motivations and realistic and colloquial dialogue. The artistic effect is not one of stories contrived to parallel myths, but of characters who discover themselves reliving myth involuntarily and often unprofitably. Rather than the artifactual sense of myth conveyed in poetry by Macpherson's *The Boatman* or Reaney's *A Suit of Nettles*, one finds here kinetic myth—myth alive and re-enacted in the spontaneous actions of real people. The alchemical paradox is achieved in that the "Word" becomes both flesh and fact. The mythic meanings appear implicit in MacEwen's fiction not because she has wanted them to be but because the actions she has recounted have required them.[32]

If ornamental myth involves a superimposed structure, an inflexible pattern into which characters and situations are slotted, kinetic myth involves an opposite flow of movement in which the mythical emanates from the real—mythical patterns are relived and renewed, often unconsciously and irresistibly. It might be explained that kinetic myth shares certain affinities with Jungian archetypal patterns in that such universal patterns are continually recurring in, for example, Julian's parallel to Christ. Most significantly, kinetic myth, as the very name insists, must be involved with process, with the energy and creativity of disintegration and renewal.

It is this notion of process which Ellen D. Warwick emphasizes in "To Seek a Single Symmetry." She cites a very early poem "Tiamut" from *The Rising Fire* as evidence of the thematic attempt to create a mythical framework in which "all things strain toward reunion":

> and Marduk flattened her belly under one hand
> and sliced Tiamut down the length of her body—
> the argument of parts, the division of disorder—
> and made the sky her left side
> and fashioned the earth from her right...
>
> We, caught on a split organ of chaos,
> on the right half of a bisected goddess
> wonder why moon pulls sea on a silver string,
> why earth will not leave the gold bondage of the sun,
> why all parts marry, all things couple in confusion
> why atoms are wrenched apart in this
> adolescent time.

Although in "Tiamut" itself all parts do not marry, the poem is a clear statement of binary vision, a key to MacEwen's search for "synthesis amid disintegration."[33]

Perhaps the very elusive nature of the synthesis is, in part, responsible for the abstruseness so often perceived in MacEwen's poetry. Only when form and content fuse is she able to grasp momentarily the wholeness she seeks: "The single, ultimate meaning is momentarily caught in the still point Art effects when it unites the ideal and the real, mates eternity with time."[34] However, the energy of the poetry, indeed its very motivation, stems from the striving for, rather than the attainment of, perfection in an imperfect world. As Warwick points out:

> In "The Aristocracies," the moment of perfection stunned the poet into silence, the need to speak vanished when integration occurred... once everything is caught, taken in, synthesized, the need for poetry will be gone. Thus, both poetry and life exist not as completion, but as process.[35]

The myth itself, "the desire to make concrete a particular cosmic view," is process—the process of perceiving and articulating "the broken edges of the air, / the flicker of forms before they occur" (*SM*, p. 6).

A more exact understanding of MacEwen's statement "I want to construct a myth" serves to qualify the impression that her writing inhabits "a peculiar ground." Certainly, her voice is unique and her rhythms and language strange, but as D.G. Jones points out, the strangeness is born of our own time.[36] Her voice is not alien but in harmony with other Canadian poets and poetic directions. Because she is emphatically involved with process, rather than detached and impersonal, Davey places her within the post-modernist field:

> In this particularist, phenomenological kind of writing the old Canadian modernist controversy between the "mythy" poets and the "Tarzanistic" realists is resolved. The post-modern particularist finds mythology innate within his environment. In the work of Gwendolyn MacEwen, Bill Bissett, Victor Coleman, Frank Davey, Robert Kroetsch, Adele Wiseman, the recent work of Eli Mandel, mythology blooms out of the mundane but effervescent realities of the everyday life. With mythology suddenly alive and contemporary (rather than imposed and artifactual), much of the pessimism which characterized earlier Canadian writing vanishes. For MacEwen, Nichol, George Elliott, Coleman, Marlatt, Kroetsch, our world is difficult but intensely rewarding.[37]

The inheritance of the post-modernist is an environment of rapidly increasing variety and unpredictability in which new forms and styles flourish and central authority diminishes. In a review of *The Rising Fire*, Ian Sowton addresses the "complexity" of MacEwen's vision and language, a complexity which is surely demanded of a complex age:

> A good deal of contemporary lyricism is irrelevant and too simply single; it is clear but not complex. Being in the midst of innumerable difficulties it gives little tonal or formal evidence of having apprehended them: it offers the curious situation of someone lurching through the middle of nowhere, yelling for a rose. But new deserts and old roses are both exceedingly subtle things; there's too much concrete underfoot, too much monoxide in the air for irrelevantly simple lyricism to survive. The unlocalized, unmultiple lurch now gets us nowhere even faster than it used to; to be effective a modern yell must be twelve-toned at least. Complexity does not necessarily mean obscurity—the trick is to be both complex and clear.... [MacEwen's] words imitate with power the complicated, crooked human heart savouring, wrestling its own and the race's difficulties to intelligible images and rhythms.[38]

Like other post-modernists, MacEwen cannot divorce herself from a cataclysmic age—her myth demands commitment and participation, and her writing is imbued with the incongruities of twentieth-century dragons and peanut butter sandwiches.

If MacEwen's prose and poetry do not offer solutions for the problems of fragmentation, they do offer direction: the optimism of individual affirmation which comes of absorption rather than negation of what is real—"that joy which arises out of and conquers pain."[39] In the essay "Exoticism in Modern Canadian Poetry," Leon Slonim discusses the visions of MacEwen, Avison, Klein, Cohen, Birney, and Ondaatje in terms of their occasional, sometimes total departure from "the prevailing climate" of claustrophobic bleakness in Canadian literature.[40] MacEwen's poetry, like Cohen's, is infused with a sense of luxury and sensuality; her inner landscapes are not more haunted than the imaginative exoticism of Robert Kroetsch's bone-strewn *Badlands* or Ondaatje's invented landscapes in *The Collected Works of Billy the Kid*. Although Slonim's categories of the more familiar regionalist and the exoticist are purely arbitrary, his essay does lead to consideration of a more widespread tendency in Canadian literature, a tendency to explore the supernatural, the unspeakable that lurks beneath an apparently barren and snow-covered surface. MacEwen is certainly part of this exploration, given expression by Atwood in "Canadian Monsters":

> The digging up of ancestors, calling up of ghosts, and exposure of skeletons in the closet which are so evident in many cultural areas—

the novel, of course, but also history and even economics—have numerous motivations, but one of them surely is a search for reassurance. We want to be sure that the ancestors, ghosts, and skeletons really are there, that as a culture we are not as flat and lacking in resonance as we were once led to believe. Prime Minister of Canada for more than twenty years, Mackenzie King, formerly a symbol of Canada because of his supposed dullness and grayness ("He blunted us," goes the F.R. Scott poem "W.L.M.K.," "We had no shape / Because he never took sides, / And no sides / Because he never allowed them to take shape..."), is enjoying new symbolic popularity as a secret madman who communed every night with a picture of his dead mother and believed that his dog was inhabited by her soul. "Mackenzie King rules Canada because he himself is the embodiment of Canada—cold and cautious on the outside... but inside a mass of intuition and dark intimations," says one of Robertson Davies's characters in *The Manticore*, speaking for many.[41]

It is not accidental that Mackenzie King's estate, "Kingsmere," provides part of the setting and a major part of the symbolism in MacEwen's *Noman*. The "monsters," as Atwood suggests, may be incarnations of a natural environment or, more compellingly, of a spiritual but decidedly human vampirism. As magicians or devils they lure the imagination through MacEwen's archway in *Noman* or to Davies' *World of Wonders* in the Deptford trilogy. In any case, MacEwen, Davey, Kroetsch, Ondaatje, Howard O'Hagan in *Tay John*, and Sheila Watson in *The Double Hook* all suggest that the dull gray surface of Canada is an illusion, that there are more subtle and startling landscapes to explore underneath and inside. "When you see the land naked, look again" says MacEwen, "burn your maps, that is not what I mean." MacEwen's exploration of the exotic, then, is not escapism, but rather an invitation to reassess and re-examine what has always been there: the marvellous amid the mundane.

Finally, MacEwen's poetry and fiction moves forward from negation to affirmation in terms of tone. Her chants of optimistic possibility, even in the midst of terror "in the hands of the living god," form a significant part of D.G. Jones's discussion of the "courage to be" in *Butterfly on Rock*. Once again, MacEwen is not alone in the possession of this quality—many Canadian writers are motivated by an ecumenical possibility in "a split organ of chaos" and are willing to take risks, "to swallow Leviathan" in the process of the search. While Jones speaks generally of this courage in relation to John Newlove, Alden Nowlan, Leonard Cohen, Raymond Souster, and Al Purdy, to name only a few, his clearest definition of the term comes in this passage when he speaks specifically of MacEwen:

Miss MacEwen evokes, and would also reject, the crude violence of place. It is a cry of exasperation, but also, finally, of sympathy. She would move beyond this Hell. Yet it is only by entering and taking possession of it that we may be able to do so. Only by digesting our world, in all its crude, complex, repugnant particularity, can we hope to transform it. "I believe," she says in her introduction to *A Breakfast for Barbarians*:

> I believe there is more room inside than outside. And all the diversities which get absorbed can later work their way out into fantastic things, like hawk-training, IBM programming, mountain climbing, or poetry.
>
> It is the intake, the refusal to starve.
> And we must not forget the grace.
>
> It is not by shutting things out or destroying them that we shall turn the wilderness into a garden, but by taking them in and giving them human articulation. We shall remain haunted by the one word which has never yet been said.[41]

The articulation of the wilderness may be achieved by "an ancient slang or a modern": MacEwen uses both. But whether she whispers the secrets of the alchemists or utters the broken syllables of an electronic universe, whether she invokes the Muse or simply empties the bag of her vacuum cleaner in "The Vacuum Cleaner Dream," she seeks to yield a mystery which is no less ours than hers:

> You are the eyes of my Mind, and you are here
> to help me see my Dream. (*AM*, p. 62)

2

The Muse: Magician, King

In MacEwen's novels, *Julian the Magician* and *King of Egypt, King of Dreams*, the protean Muse figure, who commands a central role in her informing myth, assumes the shape of her main characters Julian and Akhenaton. The Muse, who, in divine form, subsumes opposites and creates order from chaos is, in the first novel, a human magician who becomes cloaked in the divine through his reluctant re-enactment of the Christian myth, and, in the latter novel, a presumably divine king who fails in his attempt to translate divinity into human terms. The Muse ascending, in this instance Julian, assumes perfection beyond the perception of an imperfect world, "he is a human being aspiring towards godhead";[1] the Muse descending, incarnate as Akhenaton, is consumed by a desire to yield mystery by articulating the inexplicable. Both novels involving a spiritual quest, *Julian* and *King of Egypt* are complementary—but it is within the more vulnerable realm of the failed mystic that MacEwen writes with graceful conviction, perhaps because her own task is also Akhenaton's. In *King of Egypt, King of Dreams*, the sources of alchemy, the Christian gnostics, and Boehme, used as undigested references in *Julian*, are fully incorporated into a mature vision—one which evokes kinetically the mythic in the dramatic turmoil of a king and his worldly empire.

Julian is an enigmatic figure, a gifted magician who yearns for simplicity but is seduced by the power of his craft and propelled towards divinity. Continually isolated by his talent and startling physical features, he is gradually consumed by the striking parallels between his own life and the mythic life of Christ—a parallel which is unfolded even to its inevitable and horrifying conclusion. The links between Julian's development and the Christian myth are made explicit by chapter titles such as "baptism," "the betrayal," and "the last supper," and by the repeated insertion of passages from the New Testament. Julian himself performs "miracles," simultaneously inviting and dreading the worship of his audience. Throughout, there is an undercurrent of madness, of hallucination, and of hysteria, until the human will succumbs to the divine, and the ultimate transmutation of the flesh into the spirit is complete.

Central to an understanding of Julian's character and motivation is an acknowledgement of MacEwen's frequent and often dogmatic references to source material throughout the novel. The most significant of these sources is alchemy—the ancient art of transmuting metals, personalities, and antithetical properties into a unified and transcending whole known as *coniunctio oppositorum*, the marriage of opposites. In the diary of Julian, which forms the book's epilogue, the magician reveals his attachment to his tutor, Kardin, whose ruling passion is the pursuit of alchemy. However, Julian sees beyond the chemical practice of alchemy—the transmutation of lead into gold—to a "natural" chemistry, a more personal and psychological process in which the actual physical materials used become projections of an individual unconscious. This philosophical interpretation of alchemy is discussed at some length by Jung in his *Psychology and Alchemy* where he explains that it is not infrequent for many alchemists to become involved, sometimes inadvertently, with a quest for inner vision and totality:

> From its earliest days, alchemy had a double face: on the one hand the practical chemical work in the laboratory, on the other a psychological process, in part consciously psychic, in part unconsciously projected and seen in the various transformations of the matter.[2]

The fact that the mind must be in harmony with the "opus" (the actual working of the four stages of alchemy) is stressed repeatedly. Passages taken from *The Rosarium*, an anonymous alchemical text, state that the work must be performed "with the true and not with the fantastic imagination"; and further, that "the stone will be found when the search lies heavy on the searcher."[3] Accordingly, in order to rise to the demands of his task, the alchemist must accomplish within himself the same processes that he exercises on matter. It is this aspect of alchemy which is Kardin's legacy to Julian. The young magician has nothing but contempt for shallow exploration and mere manipulation; yet he retains a reverence for the marriage of opposites, the transcendent unity. The union is transcendent in the sense that a higher level of spiritual wisdom and self-knowledge is attained: a level of being that rises above the material level of existence. This self-knowledge, made possible by the integration of opposites, is often referred to by MacEwen as a secondary level of reality and is a central concern in her writing.

The alchemical theme is further explored in "They Shall Have Arcana," an article in which E.B. Gose insists that the term "human alchemist" is central to an understanding of *Julian the Magician*. The term, as applied to Julian, recalls the influence of the alchemist-philosopher Paracelsus, whose major studies, in part, centred upon the combination of human emotions and the mystical evocations of alchemy. The same instincts which lead Julian into an individual search and away from the purely objective experiments of Kardin's art are evident in his yearning to discover this human element:

> He had had no contemporaries; he had been delicately avoided by them, immersing himself in demonical literature from the age of ten— Boehme first, then back to Magnus in alchemy, Paracelsus and the rest.... The human element wasn't there as he wished it. The human element. Myth. Folklore. Bible. Kabbalah. The Gnostics. The mystical Christ.... (*JM*, p. 7)

There are many instances in the novel which support and explain Julian's fascination with the process of human alchemy. The magician uses an unusual verb to describe his own conception: "I think that even after twenty years she [his mother] still feels that gypsy shoving me into her womb" (*JM*, p. 111). Gose links the verb "shoving" with a later statement of Julian's about a trickster alchemist: "Woe to a pig like Cagliostro who shoved gold into a tube during an experiment where he claimed to 'transmute' metal!" (*JM*, p. 112). The implication of a connection between the female body and the test tube is made explicit by Julian's later remark that Kardin has "returned to his recent wife, his most recent test-tube." It suggests that Julian's birth is, metaphorically, a *coniunctio oppositorum* resulting from a human alchemical process and the "natural chemistry" between his mother and her gypsy lover. Julian himself is a symbol of the union of antinomies: he has the blond hair of his mother, the dark eyes and olive skin of his father, and to his young apprentice, Peter, he is "a paragon of manhood, womanhood, sainthood, and godhood" (*JM*, p. 17).

Most significantly, Julian possesses a reverence for his craft which allows little room for mere trickery and illusion. His magic is the practice of human alchemy: he is concerned with the psychological and emotional changes which people undergo, and he himself is able to unlock minds, thereby acting as a catalyst to such change. "Why do you think I came here in the first?" says Julian, "to show you what your separate minds will not show you" (*JM*, p. 90). Thus, as a human alchemist, Julian attempts to make light out of darkness, gold out of lead, within both himself and others. The metaphorical gold he seeks can be defined as the attainment of individuation, which reflects the philosophy of the later alchemist writers whose central axiom stated: "our gold is not the vulgar gold."[4] Clearly, Julian's goal is one of completion and inner vision.

A dramatization of Julian's magic as a process of human alchemy is demonstrated by the performance of his first "miracle." The magician cures a village idiot, the riverman, in a manner which suggests both the destructive-creative process of alchemy and the philosophy of Jacob Boehme that "the opposition of all essences is basic."[5] As E.B. Gose points out, the riverman is a variation of the wild man, a symbol of brute nature, uncivilized yet powerful and potentially divine.[6] He is first described as "a log, a piece of darkness" (*JM*, p. 32). The scene which Peter witnesses is a visual re-enactment of Boehme's struggle between light and dark:

> the magician's absurd hair fell forward as he spoke; windspell, moonwash; the figure quietened. Then Julian spread out his arms winglike, turned a full circle, touched his brow, touched the other's brow in an unknown ritual, and turned again.... Julian danced, O how he moved, manipulating the blackness somehow. The scene staggered, the light came in impossible waves, the focus was smeared. (*JM*, p. 32)

Julian dips into the blackness and pulls from it a new and restored being. The physical defect is conquered by the strengthening of the mental faculty, and from the now equal balance, a healthy body emerges. Thus the riverman represents a kind of *prima materia*, the raw material upon which Julian exerts the power of his human alchemy. As in the second miracle when the blind man Ivan is cured, the magician works with darkness and dirt, clay and spittle. He draws from these base materials a special kind of light, a whole and healed creation.

On a phenomenological level, one reason for Julian's death is his genius, his quick-wristed magicianship. However, it is not skill alone but a combination of talent, mental attitude, and physical beauty which evokes worship from the audience and denies escape to the performer. Julian has a deep reverence for magic, for its marginal horrors and "velvet saws" (*JM*, p. 115) that open doors to minds. The following passage demonstrates both his ability to induce belief and his awareness of an awful power:

> And the people believe, because Julian lets them believe... he does not force, suggest, tease, prod—he lets them believe, he draws margins

over which he knows their minds can jump, he unscrews hinges on all doors. The magician feels his power growing like a live foetus in his skull, and the knowledge of his power permeates the pores, the marrow; the sweet terrible knowledge pours through him like the worst wine. (*JM*, p. 12)

Magic based on a subtle process of action and reaction between the magician and his audience creates a state of exhilarating psychic freedom. Accordingly, as the figure who makes such a release possible, Julian becomes the object of the passion, lust, and even violence of his audience. Their worship becomes suffocating and destructive. While Julian would seek to reduce the power of his genius to mere trickery by hiding behind the cheap trappings of an ordinary magician, Peter sees clearly that the worship of Julian's audiences is inevitable:

And his beautiful beloved Julian was alone to bear the weight of his own genius while his people threw him golden garlands until he screamed under the suffocating weight of a million flowers.... O, it was incongruous and unfair... and inevitable.

"I'm going to paint stars and moons on my robes," said Julian with a sort of pitiful simplicity. "Charcoal my eyes and dye my hair and make myself look like a magician."

"You can't do it," said Peter. (*JM*, p. 41)

Eventually Julian himself is seduced by his own craft. He begins to wonder at his own lack of limitation; he confuses illusion and reality; and he recognizes that he is dependent on the audiences whose worship creates him over and over again. His desire to escape the spell of his beauty by disguising himself behind a blackened face and a sensational display of bats, bullrushes, and diminutive moons becomes increasingly futile. As his periods of lucidity decrease, he abandons himself to an image projected upon him by others.

Although Julian's death is explainable, in part, on a phenomenological level, the more sinister and compelling element of destruction occurs on the mythic level when Julian re-enacts the life of Christ. Julian is propelled towards divinity by the worship of his audiences and by his gradual recognition of the striking parallels between his own life and Christ's. Thus, on a mythic level, Julian's death is essential, both to maintain the idea of blood sacrifice inherent in the Christian myth and to support the pattern of rebirth and renewal—the creation of the new from the death of the old, inherent in alchemy, Boehme, and the Christian Gnostics. What makes Julian's reliving of myth so compelling, however, is the awareness that Julian, at least initially, is unwilling to die. His life parallels Christ's not because he desires the parallel, but because the parallel is the inevitable consequence of his actions and his genius. Julian fears the disintegration of his own identity. He fears a "lack of self-contained self":

> I create then: must I pass myself around like pieces of wedding cake to do so? Must the creative whole be split, split and sliced merely to manifest itself? (*JM*, p. 124)

Julian becomes reconciled to his own approaching death only when he is able to view that death as a necessary stage in attaining self-completion. Thus, he finds the answer to the question about necessary disintegration in the alchemical symbolism which Boehme employed frequently in his own writing:

> Saturn devoured his children, says Boehme. What is this? This has something to do with it, and I don't see it. Saturn devoured his children.... The magician eats his parts. We eat our parts to form wholes. And the wholes are parts of a Whole and the Whole has all parts and no parts. (*Ibid.*)

Here, Julian makes a connection between the magician and Saturn. In alchemy, Saturn symbolizes lead, the *prima materia* or dark substance which the believers attempted to divide, recompose, and transmute into gold. Thus, Julian, as magician, must succumb to the disintegration of his own identity before he can achieve the 'gold' of completion. The "Whole" Julian refers to is *nicht* and *alles* like Boehme's godhead. The process of creation through destruction is apparently eternal and corresponds to Boehme's conviction that the world is a processing dynamo in which fire is will and all life is fire.[7] Change and continual renewal are indispensable to the concept of completeness which is defined in *Julian The Magician* by three epigraphs taken from an anonymous Gnostic text, the *Pistis Sophia*:

> iota, because the universe
> hath gone forth;
>
> alpha, because it will turn
> itself back again;
>
> omega, because the completion
> of all completeness will
> take place.

It is the passion to attain completion in a fragmented world that possesses Julian and drives him to re-enact the life of Christ. In chapter six, "Lazarus," he insists that "there should be no ambiguity in nature, no bi-metaphor, one as valid as the other." Thus he concentrates his being on the quest to achieve a unity, an absolute unity, which will embrace all. As his possession grows he cries out in a fever:

> Alpha and Omega! That mystery is I, and I am that mystery. I am Alpha and Omega, the duality of existence, the attainment of completeness. (*JM*, pp. 18–19)

The duality of existence represents an interaction between the celestial and terrestrial realms—Julian is the spirit of divinity within the flesh in the same way that Christ was *deus-homo*.

MacEwen's use of italicized passages from the Bible make the parallel to Christ's life explicit, and the biblical echoes serve two important functions. First, they help to convey the theme of universality, the idea that Julian's renewal of the myth happens everywhere, anytime: "Without time and location, we cannot place this figure [Julian] anywhere in history" (*JM*, p. 151). Secondly, they point out vital discrepancies between Julian and Christ. For although the archetypal pattern of Christ as a metaphor for the true self remains constant, the details of the individual experiences of this self differ. In Julian's case the concept of the divinity is forced upon him because of his brilliance as a magician. In MacEwen's interpretation of the Christian myth, precisely the opposite is true: divinity is doubted and reduced to the trickery of magic. MacEwen refers to Christ as "the thin and passive Nazarene magician." "Some saw him as a divine incarnation," she writes, "others, as a piece of tinsel parading as silver" (*JM*, pp. 85–86). On three different occasions, Julian is referred to as "the beautiful black Christ." The juxtaposition of "black," which connotes evil, with "Christ," recalls the dualistic elements of Boehme's godhead which is antithetical to the orthodox Christian concept of the Saviour as an embodiment of innocence. The final and most convincing discrepancy is the mock crucifixion:

> Two men hoisted the magician and the cross. They propped it against a tree. Somehow they were disappointed—there really wasn't the least bit of excitement. The thing didn't even look dramatic. It looked just like a magician tied to a silly cross and propped against a tree. (*JM*, p. 103)

Added to this ironic scene is the fact that Julian is tied to the cross, not nailed; his death is not an agony but rather a pathetic dwindling; and his executioners are not terrified but disgusted and impatient to have the job finished.

The confusion in the novel over whether Julian is deluded into believing he is Christ or simply compelled by an "alien psyche" is partially caused by MacEwen's shifting points of narrative view. In the main narrative Julian yields to "an enclosed genius"—"A secondary logic has overtaken me," he says, "I give in and let him take over" (*JM*, p. 140). However, by the end of the novel, the unnamed narrator is so bewildered by Julian's experience that the diary, a fragmented narration of spiritual autobiography and unprocessed perceptions of the phenomenological world, is a necessary inclusion. Here, in the novel's epilogue, the final surrender is dramatized by an exchange of dialogue between Julian and what seems another being, identifiable in the diary as Christ:

> *And where is peace?*
> In you.
> *You let me win, magician? So easily?*
> *You will not fight more?*
> I will not fight more
> . . .
> No—I am already dead. The rest is
> yours—you have control. You wear me
> well. (*JM*, p. 147)

Is the Christ referred to in the diary the "alien psyche" who usurps Julian's consciousness in the main narrative? Does Julian perceive Christ as "a secondary logic," as the "enclosed" and "foreign" genius who usurps the magician's own will? These questions can only be resolved if one reads the word 'Christ' as a metaphor for the true self. Thus, the other voice of the diary, the secondary logic of the main narration, whether addressed in the second and third person instead of the first, is a part of Julian himself, an unconscious conviction that has become conscious. As Gose points out: "True union resolves polarities, and we have seen that for Julian the whole process must be internal; he cannot naively look for salvation from a god or process outside himself."[8]

Most significantly, this reading of Christ as metaphor for the true self is in harmony with alchemy, the philosophy of Boehme, and Christian Gnosticism, the sources which MacEwen stresses as much as the biblical passages in the novel. First, Julian's possession bears striking resemblance to what Jung considers to be one of the central goals of the alchemical devotee:

> If the adept expresses his own self, the 'true man,' in his work, then, as the passage from the "Aquarium sapientum" shows, he encounters the analogy of the true man–Christ—in new and direct form, and he recog-

nizes in the transformation in which he himself is involved, a similarity to the Passion. It is not an 'imitation of Christ' but its exact opposite: an assimilation of the Christ image to his own self, which is the 'true man.' It is no longer an effort, an internal straining after imitation but rather an involuntary experience of the reality represented by the sacred legend.[9]

In the terms of Boehme's philosophy this same "reality represented by the sacred legend" might be described as Julian coming to terms with the black and white extremes of will in order to achieve totality. Finally, the relief Julian receives upon submission to the "secondary logic" is very close to the sense of renewal described in the *Pistis Sophia*:

He who knows is a being from above. If he is called, he hears, he replies, he turns to him who calls him. And he knows what he is called. Possessing gnosis, he carries out the will of him who has called him. He desires to do what pleases him. He receives rest. He who thus possesses gnosis knows whence he has come and whither he goes. He knows, like a man who has been drunk and awakens from the drunkenness in which he was, returning to himself and restoring what belongs to him.[10]

What logic forces Julian, as a transmuted being, to seek the further completion of his own death—to rob, in a mood of macabre hysteria, the grave of a dead villager and so trigger the outraged vengeance of the townspeople? Part of the answer is foreshadowed in Julian's attempt to raise Lazarus. After three days of crazed chanting over a festering corpse, Julian emerges sobered but convinced of the ultimate transcendence:

"It's all right," spoke Julian suddenly with a bright reverence in his voice. "Lazarus has been raised—at last...."
"Take his body, Peter. Bury it by the river. Bury it happily, and with reverence, for Lazarus' true self, his pure silver essence has been lifted from its shackles of bone; it sings; I hear it singing...." (*JM*, p. 69)

Julian seems to desire release from the bonds of the flesh in much the same way as a similar Muse figure, described in "Manzini: Escape Artist":

...Manzini

finally free, slid as a snake from
his own sweet agonized skin, to throw his entrails
white upon the floor
with a cry of victory. (*BB*, p. 37)

However, the fact that Julian seeks a public execution like that of Christ would seem to suggest a more significant motivation in keeping with his role as Muse and magician. During his trial, Julian outlines the duties of the mystic and, in so doing, actually uncovers the secrets of his craft:

> Ivan's sight was restored because he *believed* I could restore it. . . . The mystic believes all physical disturbances or inadequacies are merely reflections of spiritual impurities. The body is merely a context for the mind. The blood is a mansion for the mind, as Jacob Boehme wrote. My clay and spittle did not redeem his sight—they were only visual symbols, sensual parables. (*JM*, p. 92)

In one sense, the crucifixion is a sensual parable: Julian's final and most spectacular performance. Instead of clay and spittle, the *prima materia* is flesh and blood. Julian's death must have an audience because his reverence for the mysteries of magic compel him to follow the pattern of action and reaction he has begun with that audience to its horrible conclusion. In that sense alone, his death is brilliant for it unlocks, permanently, a door into the ineffable:

> The people, each one, guarded in their hearts little boxes of things like gold and frankincense and myrrh, little pictures of blue-veined wrists and careful knowing eyes, and the knowledge that they had dipped their fingers into divinity, each one, deeply. (*JM*, p. 106)

"Let them glimpse a grand Unknown," says Julian, as magician and Muse, "let them recognize the possible breadth of their own interior senses" (*JM*, p. 91).

The wreckage imposed by a consuming vision of the "grand Unknown" is the poetic legend of MacEwen's second and superior novel, *King of Egypt, King of Dreams*. The enigmatic historical figure of Akhenaton, who ruled Egypt from 1367 to 1350 B.C., here provides the raw material of her vision, and MacEwen interprets him as the Muse "at his most static as sacramental object and at his most dynamic as sacramental creator."[11] Unlike Julian, Akhenaton is a crippled mystic, divided by the tension of opposites and never completed by the union of opposites. He is at once a god and an idiot, a poet and a persecutor. He is described as the hawk, Horus, symbol of Ra and of the living Pharaoh who was thought to be divine; and, often simultaneously, as the snake, Apop, enemy of Ra and the symbol of treachery. Akhenaton's ruling passion for unity with one god, for "Truth," light, and order, ironically brings magnified diversity and darkness to the terrestrial spheres of his empire. His celestial devotion to the sun god Aton is the cause of what glory may be attributed to him; but owing to his perverse singleness of mind, it is also the instrument of his destruction. He is a king who is, quite literally, blinded by the glare of the sun.

From the first sentence of the novel, Akhenaton is a victim of opposing forces:

> As a child in the palace of his father he spent a great deal of time in a dark room, living naked between thin sheets, and there was a narrow sliver of light from a niche in the wall which at certain times of the day drew a band of fire across his belly, dividing him in two. (*KE,KD*, p. 1)

Symbolically split by the light, his physique is a mixture of incongruities: one eye is blue, the other brown; his limbs, skull, and chest are hideously misshapen, leaving doubt as to his true gender. Like Julian, though less beautifully, he seems to combine the features of both man and woman; and like the former Muse figure, he is assailed even as a child by visions, "bands of moving light," and by imaginary horrors: "He claimed that a demon resided in his head, fighting to be born."

In *King of Egypt, King of Dreams* it is the tragedy of Akhenaton, as he searches for the expression of the arcane, that the wisdom of Boehme, embraced by Julian—"nothing without opposition can become manifest to itself"—remains for him a kind of impenetrable code. The complexity of Akhenaton, his hugeness of spirit and simultaneous blindness of heart, is the focus of the novel; his task of making the word flesh and speaking in sensual parables is the novel's theme:

> My tall eyes see the god. I am alone between the desert altars. How is it you can't join me? How revolting that I must try to teach you the unteachable. (*KE,KD*, p. 145)

MacEwen succeeds in this task where her Muse figure fails, largely because she has made implicit the explicit statement of *Julian the Magician*. As Ringrose points out in his review "Vision Enveloped in Night," the novel, both at the plot level and in its complex mythic structure, is built on a series of opposites: "the nourishing energy of the sun, and the bitter desert nights; the radiance of Nefertiti, and the brooding destructive darkness of Akhenaton's mother Tiy; the contrast between the fanatically religious Pharaoh and his hesitant skeptical uncle Ay; the glory of Aton, omnipresent, but to the populace insubstantial and remote."[12] These opposites are transmuted into an artistic whole by MacEwen through the drama of a human situation, through the poetry that is Nefertiti, and through the love of Smenkhare and Meritaton.

The beginning section of the novel, "morning, the sun rises," introduces the prince and the pattern of yearning for light while shunning its tangible negative, the black coils of Apop which strangle the sun. Regarded as a freak by the court of the Lord of Two Lands, Akhenaton is under the constant influence of his tutor, Parennufer, in much the same way as Julian is under that of the alchemist-magician Kardin. It is Parennufer who initiates the prince into the mysteries of Ra and who preaches hatred for the temple of Amon, the deity most honoured by the Pharaoh and his court, as much for its wealth and political force as for any religious reason. But the prince is only confused by the contradictory theories abounding in Egyptian polytheism, and it is this confusion which Parennufer cannot dispel. The unanswered questions of the prince, who works from the desynthesizing principle of the rationalist, rather than the synthesizing process of the mystic, eventually become the elusive aspirations of the King:

> "You must understand that there are many accounts of such matters and the heart must try to support them all."
>
> "Well my heart can't! How can many things exist all at once all being the same thing?"
>
> "Little prince," sighed the tutor, "you *must* understand. In the Nile there are a million droplets but there is only one river. Truth takes many forms, but there is only one truth."
>
> "Then why not just *say* there is one?"
>
> *"No one knows how, my child."* (*KE,KD*, p. 9)

While Parennufer unconsciously shapes the celestial fervour of the future king, the huge and perverse shadow that is Amenhotep colours his outlook on reality. The prince, assumed son of the divine Pharaoh, looks upon Amenhotep as an impotent stranger, a carrier of disease—"like the Nile, which seethed with parasites and abominations yet appeared on the surface cool and clean" (*KE,KD*, p. 14). Exposed to the glaring contradictions of Amenhotep as god and as man, the prince inherits from his father an acute distaste, almost akin to physical repulsion, for war and political slipperiness. To the ruin of his terrestrial kingdom and the priests of Amon, he also inherits the throne.

The first chapter of Akhenaton's reign (he is crowned "Neferkheprure Wanre Amenhotep the Fourth—Beautiful Are the Creations of Ra, Son of the Sun, Amon Rests") is entitled "daytime, Aton is in the sky." But even

in the birth of a new 'day', even amidst the brilliant rays of the king's con-
ceived sun god Aton, MacEwen foreshadows the gloom which is to follow in
the remaining chapters, each one symbolizing the twelve hours of the night.
Much to the disgust of his worldly ambitious mother, Tiy, Akhenaton's
desire to rule has little to do with foreign affairs and the babblings of politi-
cians. He is concerned only with the presumed freedom to command those
visions which increasingly haunt his imagination and which eventually
become defined to him as Aton in a moment of religious epiphany:

> Then the sun beat down upon his naked head and beneath the layer of
> his skull and touched with fingers of fire the soft tissues of his brain. He
> covered his head and bent forward under a crown of pure light, and at
> that moment the god entered him. Something crashed against the wall
> of his vision and he felt he would faint. Just as he was about to fall, he
> saw it. Not the light, not even the Disc, but something within his own
> sense. A force terrible and miraculously silent. It was the living centre
> of all things. (*KE,KD*, p. 49)

After the intensity of such a vision, Akhenaton's divorce from the temple of
Amon is a matter of course. He immediately removes himself and his family
to the new city "The Horizon of Aton," there to begin a "holy" reign of
beauty, love and light; there, ablaze with idealism, to rule with the abandon-
ment of a child.

Even in his earliest conception, and especially in the moment of revelation, Aton is described as pure light, a living force crowned with fire. For her
description, MacEwen draws upon the words of Akhenaton himself: "His
magnificent hymn to the Aton has been compared to the psalms of David"[13]

> The whole land labours, the cattle low,
> Trees and pastures grow to living green.
> The wings of birds lift prayers to Your spirit!
> And all things fly and walk when You shine!
> Fish in the rivers leap towards Your face,
> The highways of the world are open; ships sail free
> And your rays illuminate the very surface of the sea.
>
> You make the male seed grow in woman,
> And cause the son in the body of his mother
> To descend and breathe on the day of his birth, ...
>
> You set Yourself far away from us to see
> The vastness of all You made, above
> The towns and fields and roads and rivers,

Distant from them, yet at the same time near
All eyes are upon you, Disc of the Day,
For when You shine we live, and when You set we die.
(*KE,KD*, pp. 98–99)

Akhenaton praises his god as the life-giving and mysterious force behind all creation. His Light is alternately blazing, and soothing, and healing. Most importantly, night is seen, not as a force in itself, but as the absence of Aton: "When you set...utter darkness is the only light." Night comes to be interpreted not as a natural complement to day, but as a time when the land is deserted by its Creator, as a time when the births and harmonies inspired by Aton's presence are transformed into chaos and death. Finally, and perhaps most unfortunately for Akhenaton, Aton is omnipotent—a huge power remote from the common people. The vastness mentioned in the last stanza of the hymn is one which inspires fear and awe rather than affection:

Parennufer had told him the people could only understand personal gods, friendly beings they could speak to, clutch to their breasts, wear about their necks.... they couldn't accustom themselves to worshipping what to them was the "royal god" in any of his forms... he was lord and protector of all who lived—but he was not human, not even animal. Not close but huge and remote. (*KE,KD*, p. 128)

The brightness associated with the god becomes an obsession for Akhenaton. MacEwen portrays Akhenaton as a self-blinded, single-minded and therefore unsuccessful mystic whose failure stems largely from his inability to conceive of Aton as anything but a one-sided God—bright and always benevolent. Aton becomes a symbol of a fragmented reality much as Saturn does in *A Breakfast for Barbarians*. Whereas Julian unwittingly succeeds in his quest because he works from blackness, Akhenaton cannot: his actions and his personality deny the balance and wholeness of a dualistic vision.

That MacEwen's vision is not similarly divided is evident in her portrayal of the cynical It Neter Ay. Although the actual historical relationship between the two men is uncertain, MacEwen, for the purpose of her fiction, portrays Ay as the father of the delicate Nefertiti, as the father-in-law of Akhenaton, and, ironically, at the end of the novel, as the true father of the mystic king. In physical appearance Ay is straight and handsome where Akhenaton is asymmetrical; Ay's skin is deep brown where the king's is pale. While Wanre's face betrays rapt adoration, feverish determination, Ay's is most characteristically composed, even mocking. While others hopeful of recognition and advancement band together like parrots to chant the philosophy of Aton—"Living in Truth"—Ay, whose own secret name is

"Lover of Truth," remains disdainful, a spectator in the shadows. It is this distance from the burning touch of Aton which earns him the name "Unbeliever"; which places him in such curious opposition to the Priest Akhenaton: "I wondered if Wanre had ever doubted (as I've always doubted) if there's anything that can give form and order to this life. Isn't the greatest adoration born of the greatest doubt? Are not Priest and Unbeliever, finally of the same spirit?" (*KE,KD*, p. 253). Both are components of one god; but whereas one sees only "beauty, beams and love," the other sees hypocrisy, shrieking ironies, and treachery.

The chapter entitled "the second hour of the night" contains the major shift of narrative in the novel—a narrative which is told from It Neter Ay's point of view. Disturbed by reports of rebellion which slip through the holy city's shield of sun, Ay undertakes a journey to the outer provinces, and, in the dark red gardens of blood on the plain of Amki, he experiences the insatiable streak of cruelty which distinguishes the animal nature of man from the divine aspirations of Akhenaton. But even though he possesses a dualistic vision, Ay lacks the gift to mend within himself the rift between extremes. The words pledged after battle are "eloquent, poetic, brutal, utterly convincing," and intended to tear the king's gaze away from the sun and fasten it on the bitter blackness of the realm, but they die on his tongue, unspoken:

> He covered his face and for a brief instant had a sensation of such sweetness and warmth that it made him ashamed. Perhaps this was the way things should be, he thought,...quiet, bright, reverent. (*KE,KD*, p. 85)

Side by side, Ay and Akhenaton are complementary; alone they are fragments of a wholeness neither can achieve. Whereas Akhenaton possesses only the sun without its shadow, Ay, whose cleverness is "like a prison with bars, not a bird with wings," possesses both and can believe in neither.

The final climax in the relationship between Ay and Akhenaton occurs in the strange and dramatic scene of the King's death. Akhenaton, exhausted by the ferocity of his dream, is both metaphorically and physically blind, and the madness which precedes his death is as flamboyant as his divine zeal. He fashions an image of Apop, the huge snake which, according to legend, attacks Ra and is conquered in the twelfth hour of night. He then beats the image vehemently in a crazed attempt to relive the myth, and thereby escape his fate. But night triumphs—Akhenaton becomes delirious, and in his fever the only voice to reach him is Ay's. Here, in their brief conversation the pattern of the myth recurs:

"You know me well. I am your enemy who loves you."
"I have no enemy who *loves* me! Name yourself!"
"It Neter Ay, who loves and hates you. Call me
Set, call me Apop, call me anything you like."

Ay felt himself trembling from head to foot for his own tongue scared him. (*KE,KD*, p. 225)

Under the Orient Cliffs in the desert east of the decaying City, just before dawn, Ay fulfills his final command, his supreme act of love and hate. He indeed becomes "Apop, Snake of the Night, Slayer of the Sun." The King's death is ritual—disguised as his other, a woman, and wearing a white crown, Akhenaton calls upon his true father to "right the balances," to murder him in the moonlight, and to end a reign of darkness masquerading as light. At the moment of death, Ay experiences "the ecstasy a man feels towards a god" (*KE,KD*, p. 257); he experiences for the first and last time the fullness of dualistic vision and the truth of paradox:

I drew near to him, guiltily, passionately, preparing a deed which was part pain, part love—the proportions of those parts being such that no man could count them. Do not lovers turn into antagonists during their act, tearing each other's flesh for love? Do not the barriers between love and hate break down then and all truths become one?

"My Sun Akhenaton!" I cried, and I lunged forward with my knife, my whole body following the thrust of the blade until my weight fell upon him like a rock. (*KE,KD*, pp. 248–49)

What remains of Akhenaton is his legend: the intensity of his dream persisting, rising above the body torn by jackals, the empire torn by hate.

The denouement of the novel deals with the impact of Akhenaton's death upon Egypt. His co-regent and son, Smenkhare, is assassinated; the temple of Amon regains supremacy; and political manoeuvrings for power occupy the handful of successors to the throne. However, the main narrative of *King of Egypt, King of Dreams* is enclosed by two further sections: "The Secret Papyrus of Ay" and "The Papyrus of Meritaton." The division of the novel into three parts is called by Elizabeth Waterston a "triple-coffin structure," one which exploits the triple coffins of a Theban tomb, each coffin representing respectively present, past, and future.[14] Thus it is Ay who reflects upon the past of his son's life and who makes explicit MacEwen's insistence upon the recognition and unity of opposites:

It is a lie to assume there is only light, only goodness.... The holy and the obscene exist side by side; beneath Heaven is the *Duat*, and beneath the bright heart of a man is the dark underworld of his soul. (*KE,KD*, p. 235)

Without the assimilation of opposites, Akhenaton can neither grow nor attain totality; he can transcend, but not transmute. This is the lesson of Boehme, the alchemists, and the Gnostics, and failure to learn it can bring about the consuming tragedy of a failed mystic. Akhenaton is a tragic figure insofar as his passionate and irresistible desire to bring Aton to his people is noble, yet his insistence that Aton be worshipped exclusively wreaks terrifying destruction on his empire, his family, and himself. Flawed by his inability to assimilate opposites, Akhenaton, though hated by his people, becomes to Ay and the reader an object of pity.

Ay's "Papyrus" reveals the utter failure of Akhenaton to speak the unspeakable. The paradoxical nature of this goal lies in the contradictory claims that something is unspeakable and that that same something can be spoken. Mystery must be communicated, then, in such a way that it can be apprehended, but still apprehended as mystery. This is the same paradox inherent in the task of making the word of God flesh. Theory and dogma, divorced from emotion and the situations of everyday life, cannot achieve this task: the word of God, or the truth of Aton, remains remote and, therefore, is not communicated. Everywhere in *King of Egypt, King of Dreams* words are crushed under the burden of unspeakable emotions: in many ways the terrestrial realm of Akhenaton is stripped of its language as well as its gods. But the novel uses language imaginatively to convey actions and characters in which the unspeakable is immanent. The truth of Aton is spoken not through the mouth of the priest-king but through the flesh and blood character of Ay's daughter, the Queen Nefertiti. What she offers is not the abstraction of an invisible god without form, but the naturalness of love and life: the simplicity of actions which inspire words. Thus Ay says of her: "the flow of her life was from the outside in. She allowed all things to enter her, she shaped and reformed the world inside herself" (*KE,KD*, p. 244). Yet even Nefertiti is perceived as an object by Akhenaton: a woman, she becomes an ornament in his temple. Betrayed by the vulture mother-figure Tiy, she is banished from the city of light finally to hang herself from a golden cord. She emerges in the novel as a visual symbol of Akhenaton's failure to perceive the divine and the human as one.

However, Nefertiti's beauty is inherited by her daughter Meritaton whose Papyrus forms the completion of the novel and aids in the realization of totality. Written after the death of Meritaton's brother–husband Smenkhare, the Papyrus provides a glimpse of the violence which erupted in Egypt after the death of "The Criminal." It describes the defiling of tombs, the plundering of temples, the senseless rage which victimized even the most innocent. But, more significantly, the Papyrus is a confession of love. The disarming simplicity of the narrative written in the first person singular, the shyness and bewilderment of the 'child-lovers' followed by the surprise of maturity and the vulnerability and tenderness of their lovemaking, exceeds anything Akhenaton attains even in his most ecstatic visions. The lovers find in each other what Akhenaton grasped for in dreams—their actions in the following passage truly make the word of Aton flesh:

> Now I looked at you and whispered "*brother*," and the word was not strange on my tongue; it was as though I had spoken it inwardly a thousand times. We stared at each other and saw nothing but the shadow of the king our father who had made us one. Your flesh was my flesh; your mouth, my mouth . . . then we were sinking into the vast bed of linen and flowers, into a private garden, into the magical painted floor of the palace to lose ourselves among the birds and lotuses. And we were lost among the magic squares, we were children lost in the bushes of Meru Aton. (*KE,KD*, pp. 270–71)

The concrete imagery of the Papyrus, rich with birds, flowers, jewels, painted floors, and the bed of "ebony and straw," breathes vitality into the remote and virginal rays of Aton. The final papyrus is the actualization of a dream for which Akhenaton died and a kingdom bled.

The concerns of MacEwen's fiction, introduced in *Julian* and given more artistic expression in *King of Egypt, King of Dreams*, establish a pattern of movement towards synthesis, a process in which myth, unbounded by space and time, is re-enacted spontaneously in human lives. Even though the raw material for the characters in the latter novel is drawn from history, MacEwen seeks to establish a sense of timelessness, similar to that found in *Julian*, in the novel's epigraph from Ferrero's *Les Lois Psychologiques*:

> It is a very common belief that the further man is separated from the present in time, the more he differs from us in his thoughts and feelings; that the psychology of humanity changes from century to century like fashions or literature. . . . Man does not change so quickly; his psychology at bottom remains the same, and even if his culture varies much from one epic to another, it does not change the functioning of his mind. The fundamental laws of the mind remain the same, at least during the short historical periods of which we have knowledge; and

nearly all the phenomena, even the most strange, must be capable of explanation by those common laws of the mind which we can recognize in ourselves.

Although circumstance and environment have placed the Pharaoh's tragedy in a specific time, the emotions and agonies of the dreaming Akhenaton are ageless. "Wait for all patterns to come the full circle," says Julian, "As the IAO turns and the IAO turns back, it is both end and beginning and the green race between" (*JM*, p. 150).

3

The Barbarian

The poetry of MacEwen, no less than her prose, affirms "the binary structure of reality"[1] and her desire to combine inherent opposites into a harmonious unity. *The Rising Fire*, *A Breakfast for Barbarians*, *The Shadow-Maker*,
The Armies of the Moon, and *The Fire-Eaters* represent the process towards
this synthesis rather than its statement. Throughout, MacEwen's persona,
like Julian, is an alchemist accepting both good and evil, and light and dark,
within herself. As in "House of Mercury" from *The Armies of the Moon*, she
wants to be water, to recreate internally the *aqua permanens* of alchemy, the
magical liquid in which totality is born. The invocation of opposites is
reflected in recurring patterns of sun-moon, light-dark, waking-dreaming
imagery. The colours in her poems are the gold, blue, and silver of alchemy;
the midnight black and lunar sheen of evil; and the blazing red of fire, suggestive of the mythological Phoenix in *The Rising Fire* and of Boehme's
dual-natured god. Her vocabulary, whether shifting from the scientific jargon
of the earlier books to the more domestic and personal detail of the latter, is
frequently mixed and includes words reminiscent of a more mythical time:
words such as arcane, unspeakable, elusive, magic, holy, demonic, dreamlike, and unknown. For MacEwen, "paradox is the language appropriate and
inevitable to poetry," as argued by Cleanth Brooks in *The Well Wrought Urn*:

Our prejudices force us to regard paradox as intellectual rather than
emotional, clever rather than profound, rational rather than divinely

irrational.... Yet there is a sense in which paradox is the language appropriate and inevitable to poetry. It is the scientist whose truth requires a language purged of every trace of paradox; apparently the truth which the poet utters can be approached only in terms of paradox.[2]

Brooks argues that paradox can insist on wonder; that its startling qualities can awaken the mind's attention to the marvellous amid the mundane. Thus, it is not surprising that many of MacEwen's poems revolve around the paradoxical love-death, creation-destruction, stasis-movement concepts of alchemy, Gnosticism, and Christianity.

The process of breaking and repairing is characteristic of MacEwen's poetry. In *A Breakfast for Barbarians*, she writes "in this house poems are broken, / .. that image of me in you / that image of you in me / breaks, repairs itself." The recurrence of themes and images throughout the poetry suggests a constant reworking directed towards a moment of totality that can be conveyed through art. Thus, many of her poems are arranged organically in pairs or clusters: ideas grow out of earlier ideas, images build on earlier images. But always into this recurring vision MacEwen infuses the energy of a fresh perspective, a new dramatic situation. The informing Muse, creator and destroyer of language, embraces a multiplicity of forms: at his most boisterous and whimsical, that of the barbarian.

The Muse as barbarian, introduced in *A Breakfast for Barbarians*, is a manifold symbol: the civilized barbarian, blind consumer in an age of uncontrolled consumerism, and, more significantly, the instinctive barbarian, sensitive to the rhythms of a mythical reality, whose syllables are thunder. In both roles, the presence of the Muse as barbarian is aligned with the sense of appetite, one of the most emphatic concerns of MacEwen's poetry:

The particular horrors of the present civilization have been painted starkly enough. The key theme of things is the alienation, the exile from our own inventions, and hence from ourselves. Let's say No— rather enclose, absorb, and have done. The intake....

It is the intake, the refusal to starve
And we must not forget the grace. (*BB*, p. i)

To starve is to deny the existence of a binary structure, to prevent the digestion of evil which then erupts in alienation, in man's perverse appetite for violence and destruction. To say grace is to heed the axiom that "the opposition of all essences is basic."[3] Only by absorbing his myths can man hope to initiate the process of healing within himself and within a shattered universe.

Throughout *A Breakfast for Barbarians*, MacEwen gives full play to the devouring process of nature; but she is also confident that life is holy, that living can be, and should be, a sacramental experience. This basic connection between destruction and divinity, particularly in the metaphor of appetite, has its initial dramatization in a scene from *Julian the Magician*. During a re-enactment of the last supper, Julian exposes the essential contradiction in the Christian practice of holy communion:

> "You do not see the irony of it?" asked Julian dreamily, pacing back and forth before the men, the cup nestled in his palm. "A piece of the highest symbolic irony ever left unnoticed by men of learning. The strictness of the Jewish law, that no blood of any sort ever be consumed by the body—a strictness arising from the fact that at one time blood *was* consumed in a primitive society... hence the law became rigid, to erase any memory of this kind from the people.
>
> "And—" he went on growing increasingly excited, "the most magnificent deed of all—Christ, a Jew, begging them drink of *his* blood, begging them to smash the law to splinters, letting them return to a natural religious cannibalism where they could eat him, drink him, take the body of the deity into their own bodies! (*JM*, p. 72)

In many ways the poetry in *A Breakfast for Barbarians* is an extension of this irony: "breakfasts" is reminiscent of the eucharist, "barbarian" of a "natural religious cannibalism." The mundane breakfast, an occasion of habitual gluttony, is juxtaposed with its original meaning as a break in religious fasting. The civilized barbarian, sophisticated in the art of indulgence, is juxtaposed with the holy barbarian whose name is associated with innocence rather than degradation.

The first poem of the collection, which is also the title poem, revolves around the sense of appetite further described in the book's two epigraphs. The first of these is taken from the American poet Hart Crane: "Thou canst learn nothing except through appetite." Appetite in this sense implies desire, a particular kind of hunger or emptiness which man seeks to fill through knowledge or experience. The second epigraph is from Lewis Carroll's *Through the Looking-Glass*, a complex fantasy of nightmare, jumbled time sequences and distorted perception. The section which MacEwen quotes occurs in the ninth chapter when the elaborate chess game Alice has been playing with Red and White Queens, Kings, Knights, and an assortment of nursery rhyme figures culminates in a strange banquet. Alice, who often seems silly and cross in her imagined landscapes, naturally expects to eat the food but finds instead that the dishes are animated. They appear and disappear before her in a moment like a conjuring trick. She is introduced to the Pudding, chastised for her impertinence when slicing it, and commanded to "make a remark" in reply to its conversation. The situation soon shifts from a scene of amusement to one of alarm—the White Queen is metamorphosed into a leg of mutton while the plates and cutlery begin to fly and ramble across the table. When confronted with the menacing advance of a soup ladle, Alice jerks the tablecloth, destroys the banquet, and escapes back through the mirror to her own world of objective and comfortable reality.

This particular scene from Lewis Carroll has valuable connections with MacEwen's work. Both authors create and sustain worlds characterized by a wise absurdity, and MacEwen's breakfasts, like Carroll's banquet, are not just delightful nonsense. They contain their own degree of lucidity even though conditioned expectations are exploded. MacEwen's barbarians, like Alice, expect only to eat at the breakfast table. Although they are not accosted by the food, they are alarmed by an awareness of their subjective starvation, of their inner hungers which cannot be satiated by mundane objectivity. Alice, at least, has the fortune (or misfortune) to cross the barriers of time and space, to exist momentarily in an upside-down world where objective identity is confused, before returning to the surface security on the familiar side of the "Looking-Glass." Such an opportunity is offered to the barbarians who partake of MacEwen's sacramental meals. Those who eat have a chance to experience deeper appetites, to imagine and digest fantastic dishes, and then to return to an objective world with a renewed subjective strength:

> my friends, my sweet barbarians,
> there is that hunger which is not for food—
> but an eye at the navel turns the appetite
> round
> with visions of some fabulous sandwich,
> the brain's golden breakfast
> > eaten with beasts
> > with books on plates
> let us make an anthology of recipes,
> let us edit for breakfast
> our most unspeakable appetites—
> let us pool spoons, knives
> and all cutlery in a cosmic cuisine,
> let us answer hunger
> with boiled chimera
> and apocalyptic tea,
> an arcane salad of spiced bibles,
> tossed dictionaries-

(O my barbarians
we will consume our mysteries)
(*BB*, p. 1)

MacEwen's references to "sweet barbarians," "unspeakable appetites," a "golden breakfast," and consumed mysteries all suggest the original communion in which the body of Christ entered the body of man through the symbolic act of eating. But here the essential holiness of consumption is parodied by a celebration of unholy gluttony. The religious symbolism inherent in MacEwen's source material is only hinted at: "an eye at the navel" suggests meditation, and self-exploration "turns the appetite / around / with visions of some fabulous sandwich." Much of the poetry's humour stems from the way in which terms suggesting the sacredness of the past are juxtaposed with terms associated with food: "boiled chimera," "apocalyptic tea," "arcane salad," "spiced bibles," and "tossed dictionaries." The poet implies here that the dictionary is sacred in the sense that it "bears witness" (John 1: 1–14) to the divine *logos*. The dictionary orders words, investing them with absolute and fixed meanings, just as MacEwen's Muse figure is orderer of the verbal cosmos, just as in theology the *logos* is the divine word or reason incarnate in Christ. Thus the phrase "tossed dictionaries" suggests the barbaric disordering inherent in an unholy consumption.

The second half of "A Breakfast for Barbarians" implies that those insatiates who refuse to partake of the inner feast are doomed to sit at the table until they are unable "to jack up the jaws any longer." They cannot hope to fill the soul's "vulgar cavities" with an eternal cup of coffee, with concern over the heap of rusty cutlery. Instead they will "burst," explode in the midst of their own hideous joke:

> till, bursting, bleary,
> we laugh, barbarians, and rock the universe—
> and exclaim to each other over the table
> over the table of bones and scrap metal
> over the gigantic junk-heaped table:
>
> by God that was a meal (*BB*, p. 1)

The "Gargantuan laughter"[4] of the poem's last line is ambiguous: man's reward for objective gluttony may be only one loud and insulting burp.

Just as the barbarian is an ambiguous symbol, the word "appetite" implies two contradictory interpretations. At its most mundane, appetite means simply the hunger for grim "Kanadian" breakfasts, for the material objects and superficial indulgences of modern man. At a mythic level, Mac-Ewen's poems describe an "unspeakable appetite," a "golden breakfast," a

"second unreal hunger." The golden hunger is Boehme's "lubet": the
energy of the free will, "soaring to black and white." Black and white represent dark and light, qualities of the two supreme opposites of Boehme's
concept of existence:

> from the primal fire or fount of generation in its fierceness are born the
> pair of opposites through which the Divine Energy is manifested: the
> dark-world of conflict, evil, and wrath which is Eternal Nature in itself
> and the light-world of wisdom and love which is Eternal Spirit in
> itself.... [The] essence of salvation is the bringing of The Light (the
> eternal origin of all good powers, colours, and virtues) out of its fiery
> origin—spiritual beauty out of the raw stuff of energetic nature.[5]

The golden hunger is the desire to seek salvation through the union of opposites. It is golden in the spirit of the alchemists' statement: "our gold is not
the vulgar gold." The mythic interpretation of appetite is the desire to pull
"spiritual beauty out of the raw stuff of energetic nature," and myth from
the raw stuff of reality. Thus, the majority of MacEwen's appetite poems
revolve around these polarities, using concrete imagery to evoke the presence of a secondary level of reality.

The meal as a metaphor for existence is developed in a series of poems in
which it is evident that the menus of modern man are all wrong. In "Strange
Breakfasts," man is the victim of an increasing appetite. He creates within
himself an abnormal craving for progress and technology, thereby initiating
hungers in areas where he is already satiated: "we eat and we eat and we
know and we know / that machines work faster than the machines of our
mouths." In "Ultimately, Said the Saint, We Are All of Us Devouring Each
Other," man is both victim and victimizer. The role of victimizer is characterized by such repulsive champions of perverted hungers as Goya's Satan,
Moloch of Gehenna, Saturn, the Indian House that Swallows, and the Vam-
pire who feeds on his own blood. The connection between these "giant symbols of appetite" and the ordinary man may, at first, seem nebulous; but
MacEwen makes the connection with her casual remembrances of the ordinary man's "vulgar buffet tables" and the social habit of teaching children to
think of starving mouths in order to persuade them to finish their meals. The
final section of the poem reveals the position of man trapped in a dualistic
active/passive role:

> Finally, the gigantic universal spoon like something from the cover of
> an SF magazine, dips down with the shining symmetry of a rocket's
> nose-cone towards the earth, towards us here on our geometric table-
> mats at a sure, alarmingly sure angle...
> It seems that we the consumers are also consumed. (*BB*, p. 46)

The description of the giant spoon appropriately uses the technical language with which modern man is so enamoured. The allusion to Saturn, the Roman god who consumed and later disgorged his children, and who is used as an alchemical and mythological symbol of completion and rebirth in *Julian*, is here an uncompromising image of destruction. Whereas the magician can view destruction as the necessary means for gaining a greater end, modern man cannot. Destruction becomes an end in itself, and Saturn becomes a sinister symbol stressing only the dark values of the alchemical process.

That MacEwen's barbarians are aware of their position, "caught on a split organ of chaos," is evident from the tone of the appetite poems. Neither moralistic nor detached, the civilized barbarian performs to the rhythms of routine experience, yet he yearns for the deeper and unfathomable rhythms of his primitive counterpart. In "The Last Breakfast," MacEwen's use of repetition and end-rhyme transform the final five lines into an invocation:

> ...as you eat
> you delicate barbarian, you think of pigs and chickens,
> you think of mammoths and their tons of frozen ancient
>   meat,
> you think of dark men running through the earth
> on their naked, splendid feet. (*BB*, p. 35)

The chant celebrates the active and fundamental memories of the race's past—the successful hunt, the awesome prey, the hunter by nature thoroughly at one with yet master of his act, his objective, and his environment. The optimism of the memories induced by the chant is further heightened by a sense of the comic, a laughter not satirical and therefore condemning, but rather "in the spirit of Blake's aphorism that the fool who persists in his folly will become wise."[6] Thus in "The Peanut Butter Sandwich" the breakfasting couple shout across the table:

> '...Feed me some symbolisms!
> I want a dragon sandwich!'
>
> 'I am freight train, sea-wind and raspberry jam!'
> 'I am snow, tiger and peanut butter!'
>
> alas, we have too many myths
>   and we know that too. but it is breakfast.
> I am with you. care for another? (*BB*, p. 34)

The juxtaposition of "dragon" and "sandwich" and the bathetic irony of "sea-wind, raspberry jam," "tiger, peanut butter" speak of a desire to rescue breakfast from cliché, to restore its mythical significance. But the bathos creates humour, the dialogue is deliberately incongruous with the situation, and the mockery of the poem's final invitation promises to begin consumption anew. A similar tone of mockery animates "Dining at the Savarin." The persona gazes at the celebrants of perpetual gluttony but is herself a participant: "I too have come to partake of this awesome buffet." The eaters have something of the cast of criminals, their resilience marked by the poet's sense of comic irony:

> I eat in shame
> yet I'm amazed
> with what venom I crack open the corpse of this
> white crab
> the sound like a bark of protest from some pre-
> human world
> and how loudly I suck the sweet meat from the
> hollow
> of its claw (*AM*, p. 12)

The poem ends: "forgive me this second / unreal hunger, Lord of the infinite buffet"—a plea which is undercut by the knowledge that the persona's plate is piled high.

Throughout *A Breakfast for Barbarians* the energy created by juxtaposing a phrase with its antithesis is indispensable to the sense of "violent affirmation, the belief that all life is holy and the mere act of living a sacramental experience."[7] The tough humour of the title poem is sustained by a series of incongruous words and phrases colliding together in vibrant images and atrocious puns. MacEwen creates a new Babel in which all possibilities are outrageously possible: "Salome the Immortal has a lab in Argentina," and "obviously / we can stomach anything now, anything." The junk food of the present is partnered with the mystery of the past, exploding in a menu of "graceful vegetables," a "greasy cipher" of bacon and eggs, "executed fish," "the brain's golden breakfast / eaten with beasts / with books on plates":

> the bacon has nothing to say for itself
> the whole thing is decidedly insane (p. 35)

The concrete detail of the appetite poems comes from the raw stuff of immediate reality. Through it, the mythic element arises impulsively, measured by the primitive beat of the holy barbarian running through the earth.

The boisterous tone is subdued in a later poem, "Memoirs of a Mad Cook," yet even here the persona's awareness of incompletion is not defeatist. In the first stanza a humorous tone and colloquial diction are used to describe the marvels of cooking, an art performed in "dark cafeterias" by members of a "secret society." The persona becomes increasingly frustrated by the very intimate quality of food, "it's so *personal* preparing food for someone's / insides"; and finally confesses "if anyone watches me I'll *scream* / because maybe I'm handling a tomato wrong / how can I *know* if I'm handling a tomato wrong?" This mood of exaggerated hysteria changes abruptly, however, in the next two stanzas. Food becomes symbolic of some unreachable goal, perhaps love; and the persona becomes both the victim and the perpetrator of emptiness:

> *something is eating away at me*
> *with splendid teeth*
>
> Wistfully I stand in my difficult kitchen
> and imagine the fantastic salads and soufflés
> that will never be.
> Everyone seems to grow thin with me
> and their eyes grow black as hunters' eyes
> and search my face for sustenance.
> All my friends are dying of hunger,
> there is some basic dish I cannot offer,
> and you my love are almost as lean
> as the splendid wolf I must keep always
> at my door. (*AM*, p. 14)

The lover is compared to "the splendid wolf"—a phrase which implies both admiration and terror. Furthermore, since "splendid" is the adjective used earlier to describe the force of destruction, MacEwen is implying that any approach by the lover would also bring destruction. One is both willing and reluctant to submit to love: it becomes "the basic dish" the civilized barbarian cannot offer. Yet the awareness of loss is, of itself, redeeming; the returning presence of the splendid wolf beckons to a realm of fuller experience.

The Muse as barbarian also appears in two variant forms: the child and the magic animal, both living close to their original appetites, both complete in their capacity for joy. The child is "Generation Cometh":

> he grows beneath your heels
> and the city for him is easy he
> knows it from below
> old men and women you
> cannot stop him
> growing. (*RF*, p. 80)

Significantly, the child is not an ornament of innocence but a dynamic life force possessing binary vision. In "The Kindled Children" the word innocence does not mean lack of knowledge, but rather the higher innocence which comes from an acceptance of the irreconcilable opposites of nature:

> now this innocence confounds me, this ability to stand
> hours beneath the prolonged sun, expanding light
> in the exploding novum of their eyes, and
> without anger at the world's turn, its argument into night.
> (BB, p. 12)

In "The Children are Laughing," the child figure is also victim, a "prince" without shoes in a "filthy kingdom." But it is only the adult persona who feels pity and, in so doing, exposes her inability to accept the devouring processes of nature:

> The filthy city heaves up behind them
> They are older than I am, their feet are shoeless
> They have lived a thousand years; the children are
>   laughing
> The children are laughing and their death is upon
>   them (*BB*, p. 13)

The child, like the barbarian, like Julian and It Neter Ay, perceives something of the ecstasy of death with its celestial and terrestrial ramifications. That he embraces the destructive/creative processes of alchemy, the perpetual movement towards synthesis, is made explicit in "Dream Three: The Child":

> He was turning and turning and turning and turning
> outside my window on a big unicycle
> suspended in air beside a black tree.
>
> Hey, why are you turning and turning and turning
> getting nowhere fast on that wheel
> when you could be talking to me?
>
> *I've always been here, turning and turning*
> *and I'll always be here, turning and turning*
> *From the beginning and to the end turning,*
> *from alpha to omega turning and turning,*
> and I looked and I saw it was me. (*SM*, p. 56)

"Turning" is a key word in MacEwen's poetic process, akin to images that break and repair themselves, and to the process of intake and absorption central to the appetite poems.

The collection of poems which forms Part II of *Magic Animals* celebrates the barbarian as beast, one of the magic animals that have been forgotten in prosaic zoos, or relegated to the jungles of nightmare. Man's inability to recognize the essential unity of the animal kingdom is symptomatic of his preoccupation with his own shattered self. Thus, the poet invokes "The black trisexual god of beasts / ghost of the meridians / centaur who usurps my sleep" (*MA*, p. 122) and longs to hear "an anthem played with hooves and horns," an anthem which might mend division. Like the barbarian, the "holy congregation" of animals is both angelic and demonic, pitting the simplicity of endurance against the invented complexities of the human world.

"Sea Images," a seven-part poem in which MacEwen draws upon mythology and alchemy to protest against the bestiality of man, best illuminates the concerns of the collection. The poem is prefaced by a conversation between the poet and the diver, "Ley": the latter states that there is nothing in the sea to fear except yourself; the former expresses a desire to rediscover Atlantis, the mythological utopian kingdom buried in the depths. Ley's final admonition, "My dear, don't you know how deep you have to go to find a single thing?", is an implicit reminder of the inner depths one must probe to rediscover the paganistic harmonies of the holy barbarian.

The remainder of the poem presents a series of interconnected images. The philosophical queries of the first and the conclusions of the last are explained by the dramatic actions of the middle four. In the first section MacEwen describes the contrasting actions of man on land and man in the sea. As in earlier 'alchemical' poems, most notably "House of Mercury," the sea represents a kind of *aqua permanens*, a place of disintegration and consequent healing. "Underwater" the "dim figures" encounter "the perfect eyes of fishes," the fish being the traditional symbol of Christ; "undersea" one must answer for crimes committed, while the sea, representing an implicit unity, "will answer for itself." On land, however, man is irresponsible; nurtured "illnesses" "protect us / from the full responsibility of health."

In the next verse man's selfish ailments are juxtaposed with the survival instincts of a "red starfish" who is a "hostage of water" just as the poet in "Jewellery" is "a hostage of gold." Having damaged one leg, the starfish deliberately removes it and limps back to the sea, preferring its "full responsibility" to a wasteful death on land. The third image describes the persona admiring and then disliking the "amazing symmetry" of a crustacean which she had at first believed to be a simple shell. The word "symmetry" suggests, of course, the union of opposites, the harmonious totality upheld as the goal of alchemy. When the persona discovers the 'shell' can walk, she throws it back into the sea with the taunt "Now you can fly!"; thereby further suggesting that the animals of the sea are capable of 'magic' acts beyond man's normal scope. In sections four and five, the human characters are senselessly destructive: they cause the writhing deaths of white starfish so that they may use them to decorate bathroom walls; even though they are not hungry, they gorge on "tiny blue crabs." The reason given for the feast in section five is reminiscent of the mindless attempt to appease deeper hungers with the wrong menu, so powerful in *A Breakfast for Barbarians*:

> we ate them straight from the fire,
> because they were so blue and beautiful
> and tasted of the sea
> because they were so small and rare. (*MA*, p. 145)

The words "blue and beautiful," "rare," and "tasted of the sea" have implicit connections with alchemy—with the blue *aqua permanens*, with the rare disintegration and reintegration of opposites. But here, the human characters are consuming the sea's secrets blindly and not discovering them.

The final verse, in which the persona realizes that "there is something here we do not understand," refers back to the wisdom of the diver Ley with which the poem began. The contrast between man and animal complete, the persona no longer wonders, but clearly states "there is nothing to fear in the sea / But ourselves / there is nothing to fear but man." In a very definite sense, all of the poems in *Magic Animals* represent a process of logic that leads directly to such an indisputable conclusion. The persona is compelled to reject the 'surrealism' of man's surface world by praying to "the angelic and demonic animals / the magic animals more real than real" in "As the Angels." The civilized barbarian, who has buried his myths under a colossal yet mundane breakfast, displaces the animals only in the sense that he manifests their bestiality, while ignoring their magic—the magic of naturalness and totality.

As the author and chief inspirator of language, the Muse figure orders the "verbal cosmos" and thus the poet's universe. The appetite poem, at its most abstract in "The Golden Hunger," reveals an appetite peculiar to the poet: the desire to communicate the arcane, to pull from the fluidity of process a form which will reveal the essence of totality:

> How to address you, who have a hundred times renamed me...behind your fluid masks there is always something that remains the same. Not a feature, but a *cast* to which the face always returns....Another mouth is drawn above your mouth, my Teacher, and two other eyes above your own. Who would believe this ghost is the permanent guest of my blood? I dreamed I found a priceless Stradivarius in my mailbox. What impossible concertos am I expected to play? (*AM*, p. 51)

The "impossible concerto" can be interpreted as a metaphor for extraordinary artistic creation. For MacEwen, the primary artistic task is to speak the unspeakable. In order to play the impossible concerto, MacEwen seeks to assimilate the secrets of alchemy, Boehme, and Gnosticism: to name mystery by making the word flesh.

Accordingly, a major characteristic of many of the poems in *A Breakfast for Barbarians* is the idea of intake summed up in the introduction by Mac-Ewen's belief that "there is more room inside than outside." Man must consume his myths in order to reveal "unspeakable" appetites. For Mac-Ewen, who so clearly defines the dualistic structure of the cosmos, knowledge is discoverable primarily through inverse means. As Frank Davey explains, "knowledge comes to those who seek sanity in insanity, intelligence in darkness, who seek the universe within themselves, who would find answers in the interrogative sign."[8] Thus, in "The Left Hand and Hiroshima" MacEwen states "only because my poems are lies do they earn the right to be true." In "Poems in Braille" she speaks of the value of the inner eye: "I read carefully / lest I go blind in both eyes, reading with / that other eye the final hieroglyph." The hieratic eye appears again in "Cartaphilus"; and later, in a pair of poems, "The Sperm King" and "Eyes and Whales," MacEwen describes a diving eye which probes the depths of an "incoherent sea." She mourns the "backwash of vision" and demands "(how often have I looked inward / to find my own bleary eye / looking back out?)." The middle stanza of "The Thing is Violent" states explicitly the persona's fear that sanity will block her vision:

> I do not fear that I will go mad
> but that I may not, and the shadows of my sanity
> blacken out your burning; act once
> and you need not act again—
> give me no ceremony, scars are not pain. (*BB*, p. 42)

Finally, in "The Garden of Square Roots: An Autobiography," MacEwen concentrates on an interior landscape, symbolically placing herself at its centre:

> for i was the I interior
> the thing with a gold belt and delicate ears
> with no knees or elbows
> was working from the inside out.
>
> and all my gardens grew backwards
> and all the roots were finally square
> and Ah! the flowers grew there like algebra (*BB*, p. 2)

This poem combines the Gnostic theory of internal emphasis with an internalized process of reverse alchemy. The persona is fluid "with no knees or elbows"; she wears a belt of gold and her gardens grow "backwards."

MacEwen's desire for participation in some mythical body of man demands that she constantly reach beyond reality as we know it to a world that is unlimited by space and time. However, the poet as explorer in *A Breakfast for Barbarians* is also aware of the difficulty of describing such an unfamiliar landscape. Poetry, necessarily limited by form and language, begins to fail her. Thus in "The Face" she describes her art in terms of "backward physiognomy":

> I must stop dealing with clay, with faces
> I must stop dealing with poems, with stanzas
> or all your features will become typography.
>
> How could I bend to inherit you
> and find your mouth a cabinet of teeth and verbs?
> (*BB*, p. 9)

The danger of losing the essence of poetry—that thing which exists beyond the words and form—is in being too conscious of poetry's structural and technical values. Thus, in many poems throughout the collection, MacEwen in fact denies that her poems are poetry. In "You Cannot Do This," she states "this is not art, / this is a kind of science, a kind of hobby, / a kind of personal vice like coin collecting." She confesses in "The Metallic Anatomy" that "This is not poetry, but clean greed"; and later, in "The Aristocracies," she warns:

> Let it be understood, this is not art,
> this is not poetry; the poetry is
> the breathing air embracing you,
> the poetry is not here, it is elsewhere
> in temples, in territories of pure blue. (*BB*, p. 53)

In "Poem," MacEwen implies that in order to convey the elusiveness of poetry, the poet must strive towards an impression of ultimate nakedness. The process of writing, like the destruction-creation refining process of alchemy, involves not the accumulation but rather the subtraction of images for "the nude truth beneath them." The act of creation becomes "the slow striptease of our concepts."

MacEwen, whose poems mirror the fluidity of the Muse, views poetry as a process, and language as a living form. Thus in "The House," her poems are broken: "that image of me in you / that image of you in me / breaks, repairs itself"; and in "Poems in Braille" she introduces a metaphorical alphabet in which the letters are parts of the body: "with legs and arms I make alphabets / like those in children's books / where people bend into letters and signs." Naturally, when poetry is no longer viewed according to traditional signposts, it must be approached in an original manner. Twice MacEwen suggests that a poem should not be read but felt instead. This is the main theme of "Poems in Braille," in which she states "I will not say the cast is less than the print / I will not say the curve is longer than the line, / I should read all things like braille in this season / with my fingers I should read them." Later, in "The Cyclist in Aphelion," the persona becomes the "red centre" in a "state of hotness," imitating Boehme's fiery god and drawing upon the enigmatic core of the circle in which the arcane is seated. She desires to be reached; but the reaching is not simple:

> to reach me is to burn first
>   you cannot come if you fear fire
>   I want you to teach me how to sleep
>   to brand me with the violent suns of your coming
>   to reach me in aphelion

> to violate twilight, to inherit the earth
>   blind even, and backwards
>   to become a craftsman with an iron mask
>   who welds a terrible braille of poetry
>   which burns if you read it with your fingers
>   (*BB*, p. 7)

Clearly, MacEwen is most understandable when, through concrete detail and relaxed language, she communicates myth through dramatic situation. In terms of technique, she invokes the inverse to reconcile opposites, to arrive at the wisdom of paradox—for only the paradox with its logical contradictions and assertions comes anywhere near to containing the fullness of life. A poem which achieves this goal, both in terms of form and content, is "The Left Hand and Hiroshima" in which MacEwen takes a universal situation and transforms it into a personal dilemma:

> asked once why I fanned my fingers before my eyes
> to screen the strange scream of them, I, sinister,
>   replied:
> Recently I dropped a bomb upon Hiroshima.

> as for the mad dialectics of my tooth–chewed hands
> I knew nothing; the left one was responsible and
> abominably strong, bombed the flower of Hiroshima.
>   (*BB*, p. 26)

Her guilt is convincing because it is not an opinion so much as a product of a difficult self-examination. When exploring the dark side of man, which is manifested by a hunger for violence, she does not exempt herself but rather calls upon others to join her in a recognition of the deed:

> all the left hands of your bodies, your loud thumbs
> did accomplice me! men women children at the proud
> > womb,
> we have accomplished Hell. Woe Hiroshima. (*BB*, p. 26)

The final stanza of the poem illustrates her binary vision of existence and introduces Jekyll and Hyde as symbols of man's good and evil potential. The responsibility which all men share in the horror of Hiroshima represents an ironic negative unity. Now, in the aftermath of the holocaust, MacEwen sees the opportunity of a new beginning—the possibility of a more positive harmony:

> you have the jekyll hand and you have the hyde hand
> my people, and you are abominable; but now I am proud
> > and
> in uttering love I occur four-fingered and garbed
> in a broken gardner's glove over the barbed
> > garden
> > of Hiroshima... (*BB*, p. 26)

She does not intend that Hiroshima be forgotten; only that man, having indulged his darker side, should now progress towards a healthy balance between the impulses of destructiveness and creativity. Ultimately, she urges an imitation of the alchemical process which employs destruction as a means of gaining the supreme gold—a renewed unity of opposites, of light and dark, of Hiroshima and Eden.

4

The Shadow-Maker

The shadow-maker, as Muse figure, inhabits the most exotic of MacEwen's landscapes, an inner landscape of dream, fantasy, and distorted perception, a world accessible only through metaphor and simile:

> ...it's a small place, fit only for one,
> Like the thin black rib of a panther
> Or the small receding eye of a dying whale,
> Anyway, you know it well. (*SM*, p. 16)

Within this atmosphere of inherent strangeness, where one confronts both ultimate horror and ecstasy, the Muse retains his primary function: orderer of chaos, initiator of the process whereby surfaces are broken and repaired to reveal a mythic level of reality. Significantly, the Muse is both ghost and god, demon and healer, and within the imaginary realm of "fire gardens" and "fifth earth," he is, for the first time, both external and internal—at once outside of and a part of the poet, an extension of self. Unlike MacEwen's previous collections of poetry, *The Shadow-Maker* is divided into four sections: "Holy Terrors," "The Unspeakable," "The Sleeper," and finally, "The Shadow-Maker." The poems within each division form a unit; yet, each unit is interrelated, giving the book a definite continuity. Held together by an emphasis on the subjective and the mysterious, each section offers the reader a different aspect, a unique perspective, of the process of self-discovery. Here MacEwen relies heavily upon Jungian concepts, and the epigraphs which begin each part provide necessary clues to an understanding of the whole.

The twelve poems which form "Holy Terrors" revolve around the human experience of the divine. This major concept can best be illustrated by heeding the epigraph from Jung's *Symbols of Transformation*, which is taken from the following larger passage:

> It is not man who is transformed into a god, but the god who undergoes transformation in and through man. Consequently he appears at first in hostile form, as an assailant with whom the hero has to wrestle. This is in keeping with the violence of all unconscious dynamism. In this manner the god manifests himself and in this form, he must be overcome.... The onslaught of instinct then becomes an experience of divinity, provided that the man does not succumb to it and follow it blindly, but defends his humanity against the animal nature of the divine power. It is "a fearful thing to fall into the hands of the living God," and "whoso is near unto me, is near unto the fire, and whoso is far from me, is far from the kingdom"; for "the Lord is a consuming fire."[1]

One phrase which communicates Jung's beliefs concerning divine-human relationship is "holy terror." The individual may be consumed, swallowed by the force of animal nature or, as the phrase "in and through man" suggests, he may become the means through which divinity is assimilated and translated into humanity. Such an interpretation of Jung is in keeping with the chief sources used by MacEwen in all of her previous work. Furthermore, the concept of the divine as a "consuming fire" with both destructive and creative potential is also inherent in Boehme's vision of the primal fire from which the dark and light worlds emerge and through which the divine energy is manifested.[2] The fact that transformation occurs "in and through man" is central to the psychological interpretation of alchemy in which man projects his unconscious impulses upon matter, and then, through a process of individuation discovers a total being, the philosophic gold, the *coniunctio oppositorum*. Finally, the Gnostic belief that the true self is a manifestation of Christ assures that in any movement towards self-knowledge man must necessarily confront the divine within him, succumb, and be reborn.

The first poem of "Holy Terrors," "The Red Bird You Wait For," demonstrates the principle of divine descent. Its chanting rhythm is an invocation of the divine and amorphous Muse, and the series of evocative images communicate both the treachery of and fascination with the unknown:

Its name is the name you have buried in your blood,
Its shape is a gorgeous cast-off velvet cape,
Its eyes are the eyes of your most forbidden lover
And its claws, I tell you its claws are gloved in fire.

You are waiting to hear its name spoken,
You have asked me a thousand times to speak it,
You who have hidden it, cast it off, killed it,
Loved it to death and sung your songs over it.

The red bird you wait for falls with giant wings—
A velvet cape whose royal colour calls us kings
Is the form it takes as, uninvited, it descends,
It is the Power and the Glory forever, Amen. (*SM*, p. 2)

This poem invokes each reader's private demon and personal god. As long as the "Red Bird" remains amorphous—gentle, brutal, seductive, repulsive— it emerges as a symbol of both the collective and individual unconscious. It is the Muse internalized, a part of the self, the divine crashing through flesh.

A poem which illustrates the internalization of myth is "Lilith" from *The Armies of the Moon*. Here the goddess of evil, "reborn / horrendous, with coiling horns, / pubis a blaze of black stars," is the personal demon of the persona. Further, she is the persona—"she lurks in her most impenetrable disguise— / as me—." The Muse as shadow-maker is, in one capacity, the dark side of man, evil not externalized but rooted in the unconscious and indulged through man's self-created horrors:

I cannot answer for my deeds; it is *her time*.
But when I try
to prove she is assailing me
there comes instead an awful cry
which is her protest and her song of victory.
See you in my *dreams*,
Whore of Babylon, Theodora,
utterly unquiet fiend, thou
Scream. (*AM*, p. 15)

Interaction between the human and the divine, or between tangible and intangible elements, is always dynamic. In the short poem "You Held Out The Light," the focus is not on a physical description of the unknown as it is in "The Red Bird You Wait For," but rather on the moment of contact between the persona and another being whose presence is symbolized by fire:

You held out the light to light my cigarette
But when I leaned down to the flame
It singed my eyebrows and my hair;
Now it is always the same—no matter where
We meet, you burn me.
I must always stop and rub my eyes
And beat the living fire from my hair. (*SM*, p. 5)

The first two lines describing a commonplace event are straightforward; but in the third line when contact is made between the flame and the persona, and in the remaining four lines when the "you" of the verse becomes synonymous with the destructive and mysterious quality of fire, the poem takes on a new dimension. It is not a simple description of a threatening relationship, but an illustration of the poet's awareness, fear, and appreciation of the unknown as symbolized by the energy of a "living fire."

The Jungian sense of the word "instinct" is extremely important in MacEwen's poetry. Instinct, with its irrational qualities, is a phenomenon common to all races. Jung claims that adaptation to reality is man's natural instinct; thus, in accordance with its function, instinct is often at the base of dreams and mythic structures:

The conclusion that myth makers thought in much the same way as we still think in dreams is almost self-evident. The first attempts at myth making can, of course, be observed in children, whose games of make-believe often contain historical echoes. But one must certainly put a large question mark after the assertion that myths spring from the 'infantile' psychic life of the race. They are on the contrary the most mature product of that young humanity....

Myth is certainly not an infantile phantasm, but one of the most important requisites of primitive life.... [I]t needed the strongest inner compulsion, which can only be explained by the irrational force of instinct, for man to invent those religious beliefs.[3]

The undeniable emphasis which MacEwen places upon the creation of myth can be interpreted as an instinctive movement towards adaptation and survival. Her recognition of the universal need for mythology, described as a "hunger" in *A Breakfast for Barbarians*, illustrates an awareness of mature psychic functions rather than a preoccupation with idle fancy.

For MacEwen, survival entails not merely endurance but also submission to the creative-destructive processes which lead towards totality and completion. Such a synthesis is only possible when opposites are reconciled—when the "terror" of confronting the shadow-self of man is balanced by the "holiness," the completion which may result if the shadow's incorporation with the self is acknowledged rather than denied. However, in the midst of such a process towards synthesis, the poet and her universe are ultimately placed in a paradoxical position as the following analysis of "The Pillars" and "Dark Stars" reveals.

By recognizing both the wonder and the destructiveness of inner compulsions and outer marvels, man is faced with his own precariousness; by ignoring them, he is confronted with emptiness. Thus in "The Pillars," the poet constructs supports to block out "Distances, / and purple castles in the night, / Sunflowers, conquests, kingdoms, stars." Once inside her self-built fortress, she finds the "priceless loss of things," "the sweet lack of wanting," "the easy wealth of nothing for it needs / No tending and no holding." Such comforts, being based on loss, are only momentary. Thus, by the end of the poem she states:

> But now when all the world's supports give way
> As they tend to do several times a day,
> I construct provisional pillars very tall indeed
> And invite the breaking, anytime, of these. (*SM*, p. 11)

Here, the persona seems trapped in the destructive-creative process. She mirrors the function of the Muse, but lacks the creativity to make the cycle regenerative rather than repetitive.

In "Dark Stars," the persona is reassured by "the silver limits within," by an awareness of defined boundaries, and by the pattern of existence dictated by the human condition:

> Like seas we contain life
> and somehow ever are contained
> by stony shores of pain
> around us sharply drawn,
> and also the awful circle of the sun
> (though all the hands of the world
> bear us up from perfect dark
> to light, we long for night
> and furious earth, and death
> the one condition of our birth). (*SM*, p. 8)

The persona, however, sees beyond such limits: life pulsates. It is "the dark song descending / unbidden and unending." There are times when a knowledge of what we are only leads to a recognition of what we cannot be:

And beyond the freest reaches of our sight
are sterner seas with birds and waves, dark
stars, which we cannot contain, which
are not ours; and then the shores of pain
are all too sharply drawn
and also the awful circle of the sun. (*SM*, p. 9)

In order for the poet to survive, she must strike a balance between 'Holy Terrors' and a deadened environment. This is made possible by her instinct for adaptability and her willingness to allow some measure of freedom to imagination and the forces of the unknown. The persona permits herself to be a figure in whom transformation may occur: although frightened, she does not flinch at the possibility of falling into "the hands of the living God." Through contact with and assimilation of the ineffable, and through an invocation of inverse means which yield knowledge, she hopes to discover a more complete and harmonious state of being. Accordingly, in "Invocations" she calls down the "demons" of her "darker self," the "denizen" of deep want, and the "great buzzard" of her dreams in order that they may reveal those mysteries she cannot see: "(the broken edges of the air, / the flicker of forms before they occur)." In "Poem," the persona stresses the importance of natural contrasts, of recognizing inverse qualities, by demanding "Can you lose the shadow which stalks the sun?", a question which echoes the wisdom of It Neter Ay in *King of Egypt, King of Dreams*.

The dream, the inverse of man's state of wakefulness, is the primary means of obtaining knowledge in "The Sleeper." This section of *The Shadow-Maker* is concerned almost exclusively with the realm of dream, sometimes hypnotic, sometimes revealing, and sometimes hopelessly remote. Its elusiveness is best described by a line from "Dark Pines Under Water": "There is something down there and you want it told." The desired secret is reachable only through the suspension of time, place, and of familiar standards of objectivity. To some extent, the attempt to simulate the reality of the dream results in an effect of haziness, as if one were reading the poems with a blurred vision. In another sense, however, "The Sleeper" demonstrates a recognition of the function of the fantastic in literature. As the persona calls upon the demons of her darker self, the beasts which animate the unconscious, she calls upon the uncanny, a term defined by Freud as "that class of the frightening which leads back to what is known of old and long familiar."[4] In his discussion of the continuum of fantasy, Eric S. Rabkin states that the uncanny is always fantastic, that it only arises when it calls up something from one's own depths. An example of this effect to which Rabkin refers is found in Hoffman's short story "The Sandman." In this narrative, the childhood fears of the protagonist, though rooted in a very real and threatening world, are projections of his own imagination, which, left uncontrolled and unbalanced, eventually result in his madness and suicide. Similarly, MacEwen insists that evil is internal, a projection of man's shadow self which, when left uncontrolled, results also in insanity and unbridled violence. The effect of "The Sleeper" is to turn the poet and the reader in upon themselves. As Rabkin states: "We need the uncanny in art, we need all fantastic effects in art, because ... we need mirrors."[5] Mirrors shape our perspectives and allow us to discern reality. The dream, as mirror of the conscious realm, and the Muse, as mirror of the self, reflect a second, more accurate reality.

"Dark Pines Under Water" is given the initial position in this section. It examines a landscape which is a metaphor for the self:

> The land like a mirror turns you inward
> And you become a forest in a furtive lake;
> The dark pines of your mind reach downward,
> You dream in the green of your time,
> Your memory is a row of sinking pines. (*SM*, p. 50)

The persona refers, in the opening stanza, to a mirror-like perception which turns the "you" of the poem inward. The "you" can be interpreted as including both the reader and the persona. The act of looking inward can be achieved by both the reader and the persona, but MacEwen does not use the pronouns "we" and "us" because looking inward is essentially a private act. In this mirror-image the "you" is turned inside out: the inward self is objectified by being addressed in the second person as "you." The "you" is also inverted: "you become a forest in a furtive lake; / The dark pines of your mind reach downward." The forest is upside down. The words "downward" and, later, "sinking" suggest submersion. The "furtive lake" is an image of the unconscious into which the self must look. The adjective "furtive" which means "stealthy" or "sly" implies that the unconscious, which offers a distorted reflection of the conscious self, will not yield its secrets easily.

In the middle stanza, the 'you' of the poem becomes an explorer. But in the dreamlike state with the standards of conscious reality distorted, the explorer is confused—his expectations are altered: "You had meant to move with a kind of largeness, / You had planned a heavy grace, an anguished dream." Having crossed the threshold between the known and the unknown, he is now vulnerable. In sleep he is pulled down irresistibly to an "elementary world" almost as if he were under a hypnotic spell:

But the dark pines of your mind dip deeper
And you are sinking, sinking, sleeper
In an elementary world;
There is something down there and you want it told.
                                        (*SM*, p. 50)

The haunting effect of "Dark Pines Under Water" borders on the fantastic: one is both stimulated and frustrated by the poem's exquisite elusiveness, by its simultaneous invitation to and warning against the exploration of the unconscious.

Two of the more dramatic poems in "The Sleeper" are "Dream One: The Man-Fish" and "Dream Two: The Beasts." In the first, MacEwen again explores the theme of totality, and the cyclic process of destroying one's limited notion of the self in order to become a more complete human being. The poem is almost childlike in the directness of its approach: the persona meets a fantastic creature and immediately decides that she must join with him in a strange adventure:

His hands were webbed and his hair was green;
I would give up everything and follow him
Down to the dark, improbable sea. He said,
"You will learn to swim, you will come with me!"
                                        (*SM*, p. 54)

The dark sea represents her unconscious; the adventure is one of self-exploration. In the next two stanzas, above the underwater kingdom of the "Man-Fish" called "Rey," the persona engages in conversation with the ferrymen, who carry her to the gates of the sea. The ferrymen may be related to the ferryman of the River Styx who understands the transition from life to death. Clearly, they have a greater understanding of reality than the persona does, and, thus, they are able to warn her of the dangers she will undoubtedly face:

"What will you do for air?, The Rey breathes
Through slits in his jaws." "I will leave,"
I said, "And I may drown—I do not know."
"Have sense, you have no gills!" they said, "Don't go!"

I left a note to my lover on land to say
I would return, but first I follow my lord the Rey.
The ferryman frowned as deep I dived,
"But they are one and the same!" they cried.
                                        (*SM*, p. 54)

The persona's willingness to dive despite the knowledge that she may drown is an expression of her trust in the creature who tells her "You will learn to swim, you will come with me!" The "lover on land," her conscious mind, and "lord Rey" of the deep sea, her unconscious, are one being: rather than leaving one to join the other, the persona is diving towards the depths where she can realize that the two are the same.

In "Dream Two: The Beasts," MacEwen advocates a state of unity and harmony brought about by the combination of opposites. She strives for a *coniunctio oppositorum*, the supreme seal of alchemical unity, and she herself acts as the catalyst:

> And down a path came two great beasts —
> A big red tiger and a dog black as earth
> Hating each other and snarling and clawing,
> Each of them wanting to get to me first.
>
> The red one leapt forward and gazed at me long,
> Then leaned on my right side, heavy and warm;
> The dog followed after and leaned on my left
> And I felt as mighty as a coat-of-arms. (*SM*, p. 55)

The various levels on which this poem may be read are indicated by Davey's discussion in "Gwendolyn MacEwen: The Secret of Alchemy":

> A psychological reading of this dream poem would see the two beasts as MacEwen's unconscious and conscious selves, and the policeman who later intervenes saying "It's illegal to draw opposites together" as the Freudian superego. A reading in the Christian mythic tradition would see the poem as offering a "royal marriage" between solar red and lunar black, one opposed by the world of skeptical empiricism. A purely literary reading would find the two beasts symbolic of any two contraries potentially resolvable by love — "they forgot their hate in their love for me" — and find the intervening policeman to represent the paralyzing force of public morality.[6]

MacEwen sums up "Dream Two: The Beasts" very simply in the lines, "they forgot their hate in their love for me; / This is the meaning of peace!" The resolution of opposites is the goal for which she strives. But as if realizing her idealism she ends the poem on a humourous note:

> The policeman pursued me, then changed his mood
> And smiling he came and stretched out his hand;

I moved to shake it, but felt something click
As the handcuffs snapped shut on my wrist, my mind.

"*Nobody* brings the beasts together,
It's all illegal," he said. (*SM*, p. 55)

The success of the poem lies not only in its goal of harmony, but also in its dualistic vision. The achievement of unity is only momentary; hope for its prolongation becomes a criminal act.

For the poet, the primary risk is not so much the exploration of the dream as its verbalization. Accordingly, MacEwen devotes one section of *The Shadow-Maker*, "The Unspeakable," to her search for the "secret and unspeakable, divine, / the gold house of your soul," and for the words and form which can decode the dream. Her goal is to capture the essence behind the word, the naked experience behind the symbol. For this reason, the epigraph by Anatole France is particularly significant. Once again it is taken from a larger quote by France which Jung uses as support for a discussion of language in *Symbols of Transformation*. Jung claims that language, in its origin and essence, is simply a system of signs or symbols that denote real occurrences or their echo in the human soul.[7] In order to justify such a statement, he draws upon the following statement by France:

> What is thinking? And how does one think? We think with words; that in itself is sensual and brings us back to nature. Think of it! A metaphysician has nothing with which to build his world system except the perfected cries of monkeys and dogs. What he calls profound speculation and transcendental method is merely the stringing together, in arbitrary order, of onomatopoeic cries of hunger, fear, and love from the primeval forests, to which have become attached, little by little, meanings that are believed to be abstract merely because they are loosely used. Have no fear that the succession of little cries, extinct or enfeebled, that composes a book of philosophy will teach us so much about the universe that we can no longer go on living in it.[8]

France's theories of language and thought describe a recurring cycle which begins with primitive or basic feelings and instincts, progresses to a sophisticated mode of expression of such instincts, and ultimately returns to its sensual origin. MacEwen's approach to language is to strip away obscuring layers of connotation and habit which surround the usage of words in order to reveal basic sensations—in order to arrive at a more immediate mode of expression which may come closer to defining the inexplicable.

Accordingly, in the first poem of "The Unspeakable," the persona describes her meeting with an old sailor who teaches her a new respect for words. The dialogue of "The Compass" is marked by the use of colloquial language and by the recurring thought that "everything's gotta go and come back home / like the tides." Despite the humour and simplicity of the old black man, his philosophy is alarmingly accurate:

> "Look now, you be always at the centre,
> even in a big Conglomeration of people,
> and all the words you talk here
> go down to the sea, and the tide
> brings 'em back tomorrow morning.
> I tell you this so you won't fear
> and you always know just where you stand
> and how you're turning." (*SM*, p. 19)

The recurring motion of the tides plays an important part in the expression of the sailor's beliefs. Words are subject to the patterns of nature. In an effort to show gratitude for his advice, the persona offers her companion a book of poems. It is, ironically, "a pointless gift." The irony is immediately reinforced by the man's reaction:

> ...taking it he smiled and said,
> "*I've* been doing some writing too
> to get ahead in life!"
> And pulled out from a suitcase old
> as the crazy seas he sailed
> something he handled with great respect—
> a battered notebook where he'd written
> in big scared lines
> the first few letters of the alphabet. (*SM*, p. 20)

The most important phrase in this closing section of "The Compass" is "with great respect." The fundamentals of language, the letters of the alphabet, are examined from a fresh perspective. One gains a renewed awareness of the mystery and potential power in the tools of communication. "The Compass" effectively dramatizes MacEwen's wish to approach language not in the customary way, as an established system of expression, but in a more individual and personal way as a key to sensual experience which may help to unlock the closed doors to the unknown. Like the sailor, MacEwen's persona must begin with basics: she must abandon her habitual use of language and relearn her alphabet with an attitude of awe.

The four poems which follow "The Compass" emphasize the difficulty of honing down experience into one communicable word or symbol. In "This

Northern Mouth" and "Reviresco: In Memory of Padraig O'Broin," the persona confesses "I cast about, always, for another tongue." The latter poem includes the description of a family crest—a tree growing from a split rock—which represents a personal mystery to the author. She pleads to the Irish Bard, "Will you tell me later / the meaning of the tree?"; but even "stolen tongues" fail to dispel the enigma. Similarly, in "The Naming Day" and "The Celtic Cross," words and symbols provide only shades of meaning, mere inklings of the ineffable. Since the definitions of words are often inexact and inflexible, the persona of the first poem casts them away, "retaining only those / which echoed back to birth." But on "Naming Day" fear dominates, since the word that must be chosen is "unforeseen" and "divine"—"whoever owns it / will also own you." Later, in the second poem, such names and symbols elude the poet completely. She is self-confessed by "flowing water which erased / (very silently, in Ireland) / A Celtic cross."

Having explored the problems involved in communicating mystery, MacEwen seems to content herself with maintaining an appreciation of the sense of mystery. In "First Poem after Rain" she states "nor is it now an answer / which I seek, but the merest character of dream, / the least name of the nearest secret in my time." Her relentless pursuit of accuracy in the communication of knowledge through what Jung would call "direct-thinking" is gradually replaced by an admitted bafflement and a tendency to suggest the essence of the unspeakable through imagery and a sense of wonder.

Two of the most accessible poems in *The Shadow-Maker* attempt to induce a sense of wonder in the reader through the use of concrete imagery and dramatic situation. The first stanzas of "The Portage" and "Night on Gull Lake" both begin by presenting a concrete and recognizably Canadian setting. They then move outwards towards the contemplation of larger mysteries. In "The Portage," MacEwen uses the physical description of the land and the theme of exploration as metaphors for self-discovery and internal journey. The travellers have carried themselves on their backs "like canoes / in a strange portage...seeking the edge, the end, / the coastlines of this land." Once "sealords," the explorers turn towards the land's interior, abandoning the coastlines to seek out deeper discoveries. The tone of the poem is sombre, the atmosphere haunting. Ultimately there is no revelation, only the uneasiness of the travellers and the assurance that the burden of the 'self' has become too heavy:

> ...the trees are combed for winter
> and bears' tongues have melted
> all the honey;
>   there is a lourd

> suggestion of thunder;
> subtle drums under
> the candid hands of Indians
> are trying to tell us
> why we have come.
>
> But now we fear movement
> and now we dread stillness;
> we suspect it was the land
> that always moved, not our ships;
> we are in sympathy with the fallen
> trees; we cannot relate
>   the causes of our grief.
> We can no more carry
> our boats our selves
> over these insinuating trails. (*SM*, pp. 31–32)

The sense of loss in the final verse outweighs any notion of attainment in the poem. Nevertheless, despite their failures at deciphering the Indians' "subtle drums," the travellers are consoled by their new awareness of themselves.

Similarly, "Night on Gull Lake" begins with a question that is never completely answered:

> One island
> small as a wish invited us
> and the lip of our borrowed boat
> scraped it like a kiss;
>   our first thought was:
> how many travellers before us
> had claimed it, given it
> a name? Or could we be
> the first? Why
>   did it matter so much? (*SM*, p. 33)

The "we" of the poem become fascinated by the island; they begin a solitary vigil watching for something ("What did we want?") that persistently eludes them. In the third stanza of the poem, the atmosphere of stillness and loneliness explodes into primitive exuberance. The would-be explorers "dance for joy before the dawn" and rejoice in the "miracle of fire" coaxed from wet branches. But upon leaving the island the tone is again subdued—the travellers, hushed by a sense of awe and incompleteness:

When we took off over
the shallow waves next day
    our pockets were full
of pebbles that we knew
we'd throw away,
and when we turned around
    to see the island
one last time, it was lost
in fog and it
had never quite been found. (*SM*, p. 34)

Whatever secrets the island may possess remain concealed: once again, Mac-
Ewen allows only a glimpse of the unspeakable. The sense of mystery which
haunts the personae is created and sustained by the dramatic situation in the
poem and by the echoing query "What did we want?" All that the personae
learn is that objective perception and surface discovery can only hint at
deeper, larger realities.

The final poem of this section is "One Arab Flute"—one of MacEwen's
rare attempts at a longer verse form. Based on MacEwen's journey to Israel
in 1962, the poem develops metaphorically in much the same way as "Night
on Gull Lake" and "The Portage": the journey of a tourist through a foreign
land symbolizes an internal journey towards self-realization. "One Arab
Flute" combines, in a series of nine verses, much of the finest poetry that
MacEwen has to offer. Without being insufficiently dramatic, it abounds
with precise images; many of the sections are symbolic, subjective, or both;
and finally, through its development, the poem allows one to witness the
process of transformation from the mundane to the mythical, the concrete to
the imaginative. In keeping with its position as the final poem of "The
Unspeakable," "One Arab Flute" evokes the buried mysteries of the glori-
ous past, which have eluded speech. The persona communicates with her
reader and with the surroundings of a foreign land by dramatizing the theory
found in Jung and Anatole France, that there is an identity of fundamental
human conflicts and impulses regardless of time and place.

The first two sections of the poem are realistic and describe the persona's
experiences as she tours the Mid-East. At first she examines old monu-
ments, and then she is attracted by the conditions of life. Her impressions for
the most part are superficial: she is merely registering images like the "curious film, the tourist / lens" of her camera. However, her consistent use of
the past tense, and the statement of the two opening lines indicate that the
air of superficiality has been replaced by an alert inner awareness: "I was
innocent as a postcard / among the dark robes and bazaars." By the end of

the second section the sights of the objective realm are beginning to take on mythical overtones:

> I walked through pink tiles
> difficult shells, sandstone,
>   and everyone asked the time
>   on the beach at Jaffa
> but the walls had gone down,
> the walls of Jaffa,
> and I saw the sea
> through many naked doors;
>   the kites like signals
>   pointed sideways skyward
> and Arab children screamed to find
> bleached fish skulls like
> a thousand heads of Jonah
> on the shore. (*SM*, p. 42)

In the third section, the attitude of the detached observer disintegrates and is replaced by a sense of growing uneasiness about the commercial cheapening of the miraculous:

> Now through a park of palms and cocks
> I come to Capernaum, reading a pamphlet
> that lists Christ's miracles
> like adventure serials; I pray
> to the pillars standing sad
> as dolmens: Hold
>   the sky up forever, Amen. (*SM*, p. 43)

The subjective assimilation of Christ, of unspeakable mystery, is communicated not by the cold words of the brochure but by the humility which is inherent in a description of the following experiences:

> Now through a park of palms and cocks
> I come to Kefer-Nahum; the priest
> draws a crucifix through the sweat
> on my brow, and hands me
>   a small grey skirt
> to remind my naked western knees
> that this place is holy, and I
> dissolve into the scenery. (*SM*, p. 43)

Now the persona is "dissolved," unburdened by preconceptions and camera-clicking curiosity. The word "dissolved" suggests the alchemical-psychological process: the loss of the self necessary to gain a more integrated self. In the fourth and fifth sections she begins to sense the throbbing impulses of the strange land, the indestructible current of humanity that is universal. There is pathos and majesty in the children skipping rope "behind the Roman arch"; in the image of the small girl who "carries a loaf / of bread that reaches to her knees"; in the face of the small boy searching for grace before the vulgar sign "John the Baptist / was born here." The tragedy of man's alienation from the holy and the futility of his effort to regain mystery are summed up ironically in section five of the poem:

> The workers at Ramat Rachel
> have eyes at their fingernails
> and they scratch dynasties from stone;
>   no one can tell them
> that what they find in the itchy dirt
> is more than the day's few *lira*
>   (ruins of Judah's kings,
>   mosaic floors)
> for they *are* history, while we,
> the disinherited, search here,
>   scramble like the lizards
> in the Byzantine church nearby,
> scratch little marks all over
> the holy floors, seeking
> our reward. (*SM*, p. 44)

In the next three sections of "One Arab Flute" it becomes increasingly obvious that the persona's sightseeing trip triggers her thoughts. The persona's personal interpretations are, at the very least, as significant as the scenes described. The one-sided perception of the "camera-eye" is replaced emphatically by an expanded vision, by the ability to recognize incongruities, inherent opposites, and complementary negatives. In the sixth verse, Mac-Ewen's favourite paradox of creation through destruction is illustrated by the persona's impression of Jerusalem:

> To reach Jerusalem you ride
> through ribs of dead jeeps
> and rusted wreaths of war

> that line the road;
> you realize the City
> lives
> because it was destroyed. (*SM*, p. 45)

Here, also, the binary nature of existence is given full recognition:

> ...even
> the moon is divided here.
> From Notre Dame the smashed
> faces of Mary and Jesus
> watch you with ugly irony. (*SM*, p. 45)

The poet's tone is both awed and subdued—her final words clearly convey the larger importance of the city: "If I forget you, O Jerusalem, may my right hand / build another." Similarly, in verse seven, the peaceful scene of the children playing in Gehenna is balanced in the poet's consciousness by the memory of Moloch's heinous slaughters, by "the awful shadow of Gehenna." But by far the most poignant dramatization of dualistic vision occurs in section eight, in which MacEwen captures an impression of humanity's courageous insignificance in the description of an Iraqi beggar:

> I see him wave away
> the coins of pitying women
> without even looking; the
> dirty *piastres* stuffed in his fist
> are enough for the day. How
> solemnly he protests his station,
> how
>   violently he turns on them
>   sometimes, cursing, his eyes
> on fire; the old
> American-styled suit he wears
> hangs from him like a prayer. (*SM*, p. 47)

Gradually, the persona has ceased to be a casual observer in an alien land. Scenes such as these evoke universal emotions: the middle lines convey an acute impression of desperate pride, the ironic image of the final three becomes a definition of hope.

The words of an anonymous man provide the introduction to the final section of "One Arab Flute." In this Eastern area of surging discord his advice is to "keep them together. / that way / they are not dangerous." One is not entirely sure to whom or what the "them" refers, but obviously the suppression of differences by means of conformity is not possible. The poet has seen "trees that grow sideways," their bark "corded with patience," their leaves rushing upwards "in incongruous dance." She has seen "bright coins worn / on foreheads, as though they told the value of the skull"; and finally;

> ...this—
> one young Bedouin boy leading sheep
> at sundown past Beersheba,
> and the flute he played
> was anarchy between his fingers;
> I saw the poor grass move
> its tender blades, I
> heard the wind awakening
> the desert from its sleep. (*SM*, p. 48)

By the end of the poem, the persona has been transformed from an innocent to one who is keenly aware of the flute's exquisite anarchy. The superficial registering of objects falls away to reveal a spectrum of human history and emotion coloured by violence, desperation, pathos, courage, and humility. Through the marriage of dramatic situation and imagination, MacEwen reveals ageless instincts, eternal cycles, and baffling miracles; through the music of the outrageous flute, she touches the unspeakable.

In *The Shadow-Maker*, MacEwen takes a courageous if not wholly successful step into the unknown: many of the poems fail to communicate with the immediacy of "The Compass" or "One Arab Flute," or with the urgency of "Dark Pines Under Water." However, the collection ends, as many of MacEwen's do, with the possibility of a more positive beginning. In "The Shadow-Maker" and "The Return," the Muse is not simply a mirror and creator, he is a lover as well. In the title poem, MacEwen identifies the Muse as Shadow-Maker. She does not invoke his blackness, the inverse of "ruinous light": through a tone of eagerness and sexual imagery, she seduces it:

> I have come to possess your darkness, only this.
>
> My legs surround your black, wrestle it
> As the flames of day wrestle night
> And everywhere you paint the necessary shadows
> On my flesh and darken the fibres of my nerve;
> Without these shadows I would be
> In air one wave of ruinous light

And night with many mouths would close
Around my infinite and sterile curve.

Shadow-maker create me everywhere
Dark spaces (your face is my chosen abyss),
For I said I have come to possess your darkness,
Only this. (*SM*, p. 80)

The first line of the second stanza, reminiscent of "Black and White," in *The Rising Fire*, signifies not only the complementary opposites necessary for totality but also the unknown quality of her lover-Muse. His shadow, his dark mystery, rescues her from sterility, from the "ruinous" light of an unbalanced extreme. The excellence of the poem lies in the repetition of the opening line which, after the middle stanza, shifts slightly in meaning. What seems a meagre and ominous possession in the beginning becomes by the end a creative gift.

"The Return," as the title indicates, is a poem about cyclical completion. It touches upon many of the themes MacEwen explores in *The Shadow-Maker*—the inadequacy of language, the process of infinite change, the function of the mythical amorphous Muse, and the demand for harmony and love. The tone of the first two stanzas is one of loss—the lover-Muse seems only an elusive flicker in the distance:

I gave you many names and masks
And longed for you in a hundred forms
And I was warned the masks would fall
And the forms would lose their fame
And I would be left with an empty name.

(For that was the way the world went,
For that was the way it had to be,
To grow, and in growing lose you utterly) (*SM*, p. 81)

The "forms," the "masks," and, finally, the name are stripped away to reveal an appalling emptiness. However, in the last two stanzas the cycle begins to move upwards:

But grown, I inherit you, and you
Renew your first and final form in me,
And though some masks have fallen
And many names have vanished back into my pen
Your face bears the birth-marks I recognize in time,
You stand before me now, unchanged

(For this is the way it has to be;
To perceive you is an act of faith
Though it is you who have inherited me) (*SM*, p. 81)

The twist of the final verse is particularly effective. Having inherited her lover-Muse "unchanged," the persona recognizes that she too has been inherited. She is both an active and passive lover, perceived and perceiving by an "act of faith," a confession of devotion. Having discarded the masks and names, she comes to cherish the "first and final form."

5

The Moon

MacEwen's fourth book of poems, *The Armies of the Moon*, published immediately after *King of Egypt, King of Dreams* and almost simultaneously with
Noman, blends the vitality of *A Breakfast for Barbarians* with the elusiveness
of *The Shadow-Maker*. As a result, the intrusion of dogma and theory so
common in *The Rising-Fire* all but disappears—the lesson of speaking the
unspeakable through indirect means, through words which describe actions
in which the unspeakable is immanent, reaches maturity in the visual and
domestic imagery of *The Armies of the Moon*. As the title suggests, MacEwen
invokes the celestial lunar body, and the lunar side of man associated with
the destructive half of the alchemical cycle. Yet she invokes also the creative
half of the cycle through her insistence on the value of knowledge gained
through inverse means, and through the consumption and subsequent balance of evil with positive human potential. The moon, one form of Mac-
Ewen's amorphous Muse, is an ambiguous symbol: impaled by the political
flag of American space travel, yet still defiant in its mystery, despite the
permanent footprint of mankind.

In many of the poems, the moon is a symbol of evil, sorrow, and darkness. As such it recalls the tragedy of Akhenaton—it is the darkness under
which the perversities of men flourish. In "Two Aspects of the Moon" it is
the balance of light, recalling the words of It Neter Ay that the holy and the
obscene must exist side by side. It is seen first in the poem as a cup "from

which we drank / the silver milk of night" and, secondly, as a "deadly scimitar," a "sharp blade" which leaves blood upon the shoulder of the waking poet. Throughout the poem the moon is the ruling symbol of "the ambiguous hour," the hour before dawn when the "ghosts of many martyrs moan," when the "dark rain of war keeps falling," and when those who have died are consumed by flames "with an unrecordable cry." Under moonlight, the body of the persona's lover is Christ-like, pierced by the "Roman lance." The persona imagines bullets beneath his skin which she tries to "suck away," leaving instead the cruel wounds of her own mouth. She recalls all those who have suffered the "apocalypse of love" and ends the poem by stating:

> if we can't love them in loving each other
> we are unworthy of this hour and of all dawns
> forever, and have no right to bear
> the proud red scars of love we made. (*AM*, p. 30)

"Two Aspects of the Moon" is not so much a poem as a plea, "This is nothing if it is not a prayer"; but its urgency and its dark symbolism herald a still unexplored landscape that man must learn to discover through his mind rather than with his machinery.

The Armies of the Moon presents an extended metaphor. The poems form a collective invitation to journey through outer space but ultimately lead the reader to an exploration of inner space. That inner and outer space are one is a familiar paradox in MacEwen's writing: knowledge comes to those who seek the universe within themselves. It is towards this target, the personal universe of mind and emotion, that the drama of MacEwen's poetry is aimed; it is around the human 'satellites' of self-discovery and awareness that her voice finally orbits. As Stan Dragland points out in his review,[1] the genius of the book lies in the very deliberate arrangement of the poems, the majority of which are divided into three sections, "The Sea of Crises," "The Lake of Death," and "The Lake of Dreams." Each of these sections explores a particular theme or state of mind; and each represents one step in the journey towards self-knowledge. They are followed by the nine-poem "The Nine Arcana of the Kings," which Dragland considers both ornamental and functional. Finally, the collection is framed by the beginning title poem and the concluding poem "Apollo Twelve." Their imagery, derived largely from space travel, helps to sustain the original metaphor of the poems as a unified whole. It is obvious that MacEwen is striving consciously to guide her reader through the journey in order that the significance of the final poem can be properly appreciated. The guidance, however, is developed smoothly from the merit of the poems themselves rather than from epigraphs such as those she uses in *The Shadow-Maker*, many of which require a specialized knowledge before their importance can be fully grasped. When *The Armies of the Moon* is read with its overlying pattern of continuity in mind, the intensity of its poetic experience cannot fail to be heightened.

In the first poem, "The Armies of the Moon," MacEwen visualizes an impending clash between the "unseen silver armies" and the blind earthmen. Their battleground, "the gorgeous anonymous moon," possesses a mystery which is unspoiled by the golf balls of the earth's explorers and untouched by the frenzied gathering of "white rocks and sand." The lunar forces "invisible and silver as swords turned sideways" gather in "The Sea of Crises" patiently waiting for "earthrise and the coming of man." Their ethereal and ageless qualities are well established in the second stanza:

> they have always been there increasing their numbers
> at the foot of dim rills, all around and under
> the ghostly edges where moonmaps surrender
> and hold out white flags to the night. (*AM*, p. 1)

The eager earthmen rudely intrude into this lunar landscape. Significantly, they are unable to see the silver edges of the moon's army (silver being the colour associated with the alchemical god Mercurius, the symbol of synthesis and totality) and, accordingly, are presumed blind by the lunar forces. In the last two stanzas of the poem, the persona promises that confrontation between the opposing forces is inevitable. The unseen armies embody the qualities of myth; thus, on a symbolic level, the inevitable confrontation may be interpreted as one between myth and technology.

> in the Lake of Death there will be a showdown;
> men will be powder, they will go down under
> the swords of the unseen silver armies,
> become one with the gorgeous anonymous moon.
>
> none of us will know what caused the crisis
> as the lunar soldiers reluctantly disband
> and return to their homes in the Lake of Dreams
> weeping quicksilver tears for the blindness of man.
>
> (*AM*, p. 1)

The earthmen are destroyed in "The Lake of Death" by an unseen band of soldiers; yet it is only by succumbing to their opponent's sword that the earthmen can finally enter the landscape of the moon. In the last stanza, the lunar army mourns its absurdly easy victory. Their home is "the Lake of Dreams," the landscape of possibility where man, ineffectual and symbolically blind, cannot hope to follow.

The importance of this poem, though powerful in itself, lies, as Dragland recognizes, in its effort to set up "the finite beginning and the infinite becoming 'end' of the journey through inner space which the mind takes through the book."[2] Here man stands on the rims of the craters of discovery, and the army he must struggle with is a "ghostly" and "invisible" manifestation of myth which he cannot see because he lacks dualistic vision. In the successive stanzas of the poem, MacEwen defines the focus of each of the collection's three sections which follow this introductory poem: "a gathering of forces," "earthrise" in the "Sea of Crises"; "showdown," destruction, in "The Lake of Death"; and ultimately "quicksilver tears," the creation which stems from destruction, in "The Lake of Dreams." The use of the word "silver," repeated four times, is associated both with the lunar and traditionally mysterious celestial body and with the ancient study of alchemy. In order for the earthman to have any chance against the ethereal army he must necessarily confront negatives and combine opposites. He must alter his state of blindness in order that he, too, at one with the silver armies, may glimpse "The Lake of Dreams."

In "The Sea of Crises," the first major section, MacEwen creates and sustains a sense of having lost something valid, a sense of precariousness, and a suspicion of lurking myths and marvels that have been suppressed by dreary routine. The second stanza of "A Lecture to the Flat Earth Society" seems to epitomize the wariness of "The Sea of Crises":

> My God I've lived all my life right here
> On the Rim, the Brink, the Final Boundary of fear
> With the long flat continents of dreams behind me
> And nothing ahead but the sweet and terrible Night
> I long to fall into, but do not dare. (*AM*, p. 20)

Man is aware of different dimensions, of dim possibilities, but reluctant to explore them. Always it is the "Final Boundary" which both tempts and terrifies the "I" of the poems.

With only a few exceptions all of the poems in this section are arranged organically: although each is complete individually, each leads naturally into the next. This arrangement in itself is suggestive of the process of alchemy, in which totality is achieved only after the successful completion of a series of smaller steps. For example, in the first two poems "The Hunt" and "I have Mislaid Something," the poet, as the titles suggest, is aware of something which constantly evades her: "I have mislaid many places / in this house without history / there are so many places for places to hide." In the third poem "Meditations of a Seamstress (1)" this sense of loss is blended with one of precariousness:

> (Something vital is at stake,
> the Lost Stitch or the Ultimate Armhole,
> I don't know what) and hour after hour
> on the venerable Singer
> I make strong seams for my dresses
> and my world. (*AM*, p. 8)

The persona feels threatened by a strange compulsion she cannot name. As the poem progresses, the seamstress assumes personal responsibility for the fragile nature of the entire world:

> I know somehow I'm fighting time
> and if it's not all done by nightfall
> everything will come apart again;
> continental shelves will slowly drift into the sea
> and earthquakes will tear wide open
> the worn-out patches of Asia. (*AM*, p. 8)

Finally, by the last ten lines, her routine occupation is translated into a mythic experience. Sewing becomes a metaphor for the countless domestic pressures, which by becoming habits, offer temporary protection for those "at the hem of the world":

> Dusk, a dark needle, stabs the city
> and I get visions of chasing fiery spools of thread
> mile after mile over highways and fields
> until I inhabit some place at the hem of the world
> where all the long blue draperies
> of skies and rivers wind;
>   spiders' webs describe
> the circling of their frail thoughts forever;
> everything fits at last and someone has lined
> the thin fabric of this life I wear with grass. (*AM*, p. 9)

The image of the spider with its infinite and delicate webbings is an effective visual image of mankind's efforts to impress patterns of security upon his hazardous environment, upon the "thin fabric of life." It is important to note that the feelings of appalling vulnerability which dominate the persona in the central section of the poem have, by the end, been alleviated: even though she knows that her security is only temporary, the persona cannot yet disregard it.

"Meditations of a Seamstress (2)," together with a later poem, "Hypnos" from "The Lake of Dreams," and a short story, "The Oarsman and the Seamstress" from *Noman*, form a trilogy which depicts the need both to combine opposites and to surrender to the unknown. In the short story, the heroine, who remains nameless, wishes to enter the dreams of her sleeping lover, Constantine. While sewing a dress from a sheath of red velvet, she considers that her own state of waking reality allows her an advantage over her lover, while it simultaneously isolates her from him:

> Constantine was still asleep, and she hoped the rustling of the paper pattern wouldn't wake him. She loved to watch him while he slept, perhaps because in his sleep he no longer possessed himself, he was a lost being, a kind of orphan, suspended in another time and connected only by the thinnest of threads to his own consciousness. She loved to watch him while he slept, perhaps because it was then that she could enjoy the illusion of actually knowing him, knowing him in his *otherness*, his state of being other than her. His sleep alienated her and paradoxically, drew her closer to him. (*N*, p. 48)

The state of "otherness" is both inviolate and exotic: as in the earlier lover-Muse poems, it is a quality which MacEwen reveres.

The seamstress continues to measure her material while musing on the dream fantasies of her companion until his physical presence finally begins to overpower her. She is captivated by his body, by "the strong lyrical line of his side," by "an anatomy so breathtakingly different from her own." She is frustrated by her inability to "possess" him, and by the impossibility of accompanying him in the sleep where she imagines him manning the oars of a golden Byzantine ship. Longing to unite her body and spirit with his by crossing over the boundary of his altered consciousness, she eventually abandons her activity and her state of wakefulness:

> Suddenly she realized that if she tried to sew anything today she'd go mad. Or maybe she wouldn't which would be worse. So she threw off her housecoat, took the great piece of dark red velvet and quietly climbed into bed beside him. Then she gently eased all the sheets and blankets off the bed and onto the floor, and covered her naked body and his naked body with the dark red velvet.
>
> *Is there room for a woman on your ship?* she whispered into his ear. *I'll stow away, no-one will see me, I'll be hidden by dark red velvet. Take me with you, Constantine.* (*N*, p. 51)

The shapeless but exquisite velvet becomes a symbol of both her hope for unity and her submission to mystery.

The first six lines of "Meditations of a Seamstress (2)" echo the thoughts of the heroine in the short story who desires her clothes to be elegantly self-confessing:

> I dream impossible clothes which will confess me
> and fall apart miraculous as the Red Sea
> to reveal to you the stunning contours of my
> mind (you who wear the world with a grace
> I will never achieve, invisibly,
> like the arcane garment of the emperor). (*AM*, p. 10)

In the final stanza, the poet imitates the eager vulnerability of the Seamstress; where one chooses red velvet as a symbol of her desire for unity, the other remembers a simple robe which opened like a door onto the mystery of her nakedness:

> Only one dress I made ever came out right—
> (it will never happen that way again);
> all the way down the front of it
> where it opens from the collar to the hem
> I sewed the signs of Athens,
> a row of obsolete but perfect keys
> on a strip of black and gold,
> with which you may, O naked emperor,
> enter and decode my world. (*AM*, p. 10)

This poem utilizes, of course, the child's story of "The Emperor With No Clothes"; but, here, the emperor enjoys the status of a Muse figure. His 'nakedness' is a matter of perspective—to be clothed is to be false, to be retreating behind the obvious.

The second poem, "Hypnos," which takes its title from the Greek god of sleep, mirrors the tenderness of "The Oarsman and the Seamstress" and captures the essence of the "otherness" which the persona attributes to Constantine. Here, however, there is no hope of violating his sleep: "it offers me no entry and no alibi." Whereas Constantine seems almost helpless in dreams like an "orphan," the lover in "Hypnos" is vaguely frightening, "for in sleep he is powerful / as a withheld word." The persona can only pay homage to his mystery:

> He lies there accomplished and unknown,
> his limbs arranged by passion and by art,
> a fluid beauty he inhabits all alone.

The dark bird of war is dormant in his loins
and prophets reside in the seeds of his kiss;
    the generations of his mouth are legion
    yet his body is inviolably his.
He may lie, he may live there forever
and I can say nothing of the meaning of this sleeper
                         (*AM*, p. 57)

Described as both "accomplished" and "unknown," the sleeper is a Muse figure who is both destructive and creative in his sexuality. His "fluid beauty" is the beauty of process, and the totality of the alchemical god Mercurius. The persona finds that his beauty renders her speechless, "I can say nothing of the meaning of this sleeper." Yet her tone communicates the reverence necessary for her to move toward his realm. Read as a unit, "Hypnos," "Meditations of a Seamstress (2)," and "The Oarsman and the Seamstress" illustrate MacEwen's dominant themes of process and totality, and demonstrate her ability to write well in different literary forms. Most significantly, in their attention to detail and dramatic setting, they give credibility to the renewal of myth.

Many of the poems in "The Sea of Crises" focus upon a process of gathering, an action similar to the spacemen's frenzied gathering of objects in the title poem. The desire is for enclosure, for the consumption of the unknown found also in MacEwen's appetite poems. And, as in *A Breakfast for Barbarians*, it is material objects rather than mystery which are finally consumed. Man yearns for myth but cannot digest its dangerous possibilities. Thus, in a key poem "Phobos," MacEwen writes:

Last week lightning clove the mighty tree
outside my house, and the leaves turned in
surrendering their white sides; I learned
that lightning cleaves what it most loves
and cuts in half what it means to caress (*AM*, p. 24)

The opposites of love and death, and creation and destruction, implied in this poem are echoed in the appetite poems "Dining at the Savarin" and "Memoirs of a Mad Cook" and, in modified form, in "The Vacuum Cleaner Dream." Engaged in a frenzy of domesticity, the persona sweeps up the world "with a sickening efficiency" and discovers in the bag of her "blind machine," "the sleeping body of my love."

Finally, in "The Holy Burlesque," the Muse figure dances into secret knowledge in a performance which epitomizes the essential brilliance and horror of embracing myth. MacEwen employs colloquial language and estab-

lishes a comfortable atmosphere which is soon undercut by the subtle introduction of deeper realities. The Greek dancer, Laki, wriggles seductively
across the nightclub stage "crying whoopah! and ellah! / in the best tradition." His dance at first serves only to parody the predictable grindings of
"the large mammalian thing / who keeps falling over backwards / into her
seventh orange veil." But the casual laughter elicited by the poem's first
section quickly dissolves into a kind of protective hysteria in the last ten
lines. Laki's eyes promise to reveal unspeakable secrets, the "Oh so lovely
sins / of Sodom and Athens and East Toronto" which have long since been
suppressed. The bathos created by the unlikely conjunction and anti-climac-
tic ordering of the three cities signals a change of mood. Laki's dance threat-
ens the gaudy nightclub madness and reveals another possibility:

> if we didn't laugh for heaven's sake,
> if there was one minute of silence
> in the Greek nightclub down the street
> Laki's laugh would sound so shrill and pure
> we'd fall over backwards
> into our *retzinas* or our seventh orange beer
> and rise, and repossess the stage
> we occupied before two thousand years.
> Our lies in a blaze of orange veils would vanish
> and the very gods might reappear. (*AM*, p. 17)

The characters' masks are shattered; they fall "backwards" only to "rise"
and "repossess." In a re-enactment of the destruction-creation cycle, the
protective lies of the persona disappear, allowing for a possible reappearance
of the gods. It is evident from the persona's tone of hysteria that contemplation of such a confrontation is as paralyzing as the confrontation between
man and god in the most compelling poems from *The Shadow-Maker*. Frank
Davey provides the connection between this poem and the earlier collection,
by concluding his assessment of *The Armies of the Moon* with the recollection
of the previous epigraph: "It is a fearful thing to fall into the hands of the
living god."[3]

In "The Lake of Death," the central section of *The Armies of the Moon*,
MacEwen focuses upon the horrific aspect of the moon symbol—the moon
which terrifies Akhenaton in *King of Egypt, King of Dreams*, and which rules
over the tangible blackness of night where "five gods waited with knives to
hack living souls to shreds" (p. 102). In "The Lake of Death" the emphasis
shifts from gods to man. Man indulges that part of his being symbolized by
the moon to such an extent that his darkness overpowers the reconciling light
of the sun; he has eclipsed his own potential for binary vision and hacked

to shreds the possibility of achieving totality. Thus, in "The Telescope Turned Inward," MacEwen urges a confrontation with man's most inner and shadowy self, with "imponderable agonies" which have too long been ignored. She creates a mood in which "the lens like your dead eye / which fell away from stars / turns to the vivid zero / of your dreams." Those horrors which previously have lurked on the periphery of the conscious must now be pushed forward under the glaring spotlight of responsibility for only by considering both the negative and positive aspects of his being can man perceive with the fullness of a vision which enables him to realize an inherent unity in his dualistic universe.

That man is individually and collectively responsible for his own destruction is a familiar theme in MacEwen's work. In *The Trojan Women*, Hecuba mourns "Nothing is alive but the hungry dark"; yet it is the lesson of the play that the dark is internal:

> I will tell you something I've only recently
> learned—
> war is blood and blood and blood,
> war is babies falling
> from the cradles of the sky.
> War is the final nightmare.
> The last sick page in a long sick story.
> War is something that *we* do—
> All of us, all of us. (*TW*, p. 65)

This concept of internalized violence is echoed in the third stanza of "The Other Underground":

> you have not noticed that all wars
> are happening inside my head,
> you have not asked me to get out of Vietnam,
> the conflagration which is the Asia of my mind
> where I commit, alone,
> the atrocities of my time. (*AM*, 34)

The persona is not innocent of those crimes and nightmares for which she condemns others. She admits to her own "dark committees" of the soul, to her own "guerillas" of guilt, to her own "bloody hands." In the fourth stanza of the poem, which is reminiscent of an earlier selection from *A Breakfast for Barbarians*, she assumes responsibility for Hiroshima, seeing in that act a kind of reverse alchemy:

> tell me what the dark committees of my soul are
>   plotting
> and where the guerillas of my guilt are hiding
>   out—
> for I remember that the cockpit of the plane
> was silent in Hiroshima,
> as silent as my skull, O silent
> was my skull before eyes bled from heads,
> dripped out or melted inward,
> before the man sitting in the sun somewhere
> *dissolved* and left the black atomic shadow
> of his soul upon the stairs. (*AM*, p. 34)

The manifestations of brutality become the "prima materia" for a reverse alchemical process which transforms sun into shadow, and light into dark. Instead of gathering opposites, evil shatters them; man dissolves rather than fulfills his potential for completeness.

In the final section of "The Other Underground," MacEwen employs the symbolism of the moon to expose the very core of evil, and she shudders under the responsibility of its telling:

> the midnights lit by warlight, scarlet stars,
> the sheer hallucination of our wars
> have somehow grown from small hurts, symbolic
> murders,
> and the tyranny is with us everyday
> in our small cruel lies,
> in our turning away from love,
> and the Enemy is where he always was—
> in the bleak lunar landscapes of our mirrors.
>
> I'm so far underground you cannot find me,
> hating the untellable which must get told,
> trying to read the monthly Morse-code of the moon,
> these urgent letters to the world. (*AM*, p. 35)

Here evil is a private, habitual "tyranny." While its ugliness is often recognized only in spectacular eruptions, its roots grow in the most trivial of occurrences. It is appallingly ordinary, appallingly widespread. Here, too, the moon is a mirror just as the Muse is a mirror in *The Shadow-Maker*: our own reflection is inescapable.

Perhaps the strongest poem of "The Lake of Death" is "The Film," in which the external "silver screen" of the movies is used as a metaphor for a 'human' screen upon which man impresses the panoramic spectacles of his lunar self. In the first stanza, the persona watches man's perverse performance in the "dark theatres" of her own blood and equates the screen with human life: "The fervent curtains fall apart / and the silver screen is skin." The last stanza depicts explicitly the unnatural tendency for the indulgence in evil—an indulgence which transforms the negative or lunar potential of man into a narcotic drama:

> I think that when you raise your hand
> against those walls
> your flesh becomes a screen,
>   the drama unfolds
> along your fingers
> and across your open palm the armies run
> and down your veins their false blood falls;
>   I want to tell you—
> Look this is the kind of war nobody needs.
> But now the images have claimed your face,
>   you are alive with lies and legends,
> the silver reel unravels in your skull,
> the dark film roars forever down your blood.
>
> (*AM*, p. 43)

Man becomes not only the instigator and perpetrator of darkness, but also the victim of its unleashed strength. Again, MacEwen stresses that evil is an internal sickness, not an external accident.

One wonders where MacEwen can possibly turn after she has scrutinized the abyss, how she can possibly re-establish the healing processes of alchemy and begin anew the coupling of opposites, or how she can again inform the moon with a holier beauty. The answer is provided by "A Letter to Charos," a poem in which she invokes the mythological ferryman of the River Styx, "Lord of the midnight river" and death, in order to explain the illusionary and dissolving meanings of existence. In the middle stanzas, the persona's life is hopelessly amorphous: her "silver hands like fish / slip away" from her "lover's flesh"; death is a "liquid kiss"; and living is "like a coin tossed into a midnight fountain." All of these images suggest the dissolving process in alchemy. Finally, desperately, the persona asks: "was it all a magic act of sun and water / was there something else I should have done instead." Her own answer directly recalls the crucial question explored throughout *Noman*:

into whose future am I moving

my thighs, all silver with his seed
are sleek for swimming,
I see the aqueducts of death ahead (*AM*, p. 45)

Having gorged on perversity and wallowed in darkness, man finds that his salvation is the 'death' which carries within it the "seed" of rebirth. The explicit sexual imagery promises rejuvenation; and with this tentative hope, MacEwen approaches the final phase of her exploration, "The Lake of Dreams."

The journey begins with an invocation of the Muse/Mercurius figure, "composite god" of the "philosophical gold" in "The Golden Hunger." The moon becomes not a symbol of hate or of crippled potential, but a passive witness to the poet's effort for achievement. Earlier in the poem, the persona sees the moon "yellow and terrifically full" which implies that its "silver sheen" has mellowed. Its blade-like curve, which in "The Lake of Death" suggests a weapon, has achieved the completeness of a circle. Having once opened "the savage flower of the mind," MacEwen cannot ignore the more sinister aspects of the moon. Instead she seeks for "a reconciling light which will subsume rather than oppose the darkness."[4]

In the next two poems the synthesizing processes of alchemy are further dramatized, although it should be noted that *The Armies of the Moon*, in comparison with some of MacEwen's earlier publications, integrates the alchemical source material more fully. In "Jewellery" the symbolic gold of alchemy is inherent in the persona's assortment of bracelets, earrings, and rings. Within this "glittering prison" she is a willing captive, for her greatest desire is to submit to the healing light which the gold represents:

I wear it more to be its captive
than to captivate; I want
to be the prisoner of gold,
to hear my voice break through
the chain which holds my song
in check, (*AM*, p. 53)

Similarly, in "House of Mercury," the persona states: "Leave me be, I want to be water." She expresses her desire that "all those who come to me / should wear the blue metal or the quick / silver of the sea which glints its mineral / histories." This reflects MacEwen's own wish to metaphorically re-create within herself and her readers the mercurial *aqua permanens* in which all material is dissolved so that it may be harmoniously recombined. The *aqua permanens* is the liquid from which the healing god Mercurius traditionally springs; thus, by desiring to become the transmuting agent, MacEwen's persona expresses a larger desire to be reunited with the Muse. The later poem "Hypnos," which has already been discussed, also alludes to Mercurius. The sleeper possesses a "fluid beauty," and the sexual imagery connected with his loins, his kiss, and his mouth carries a promise of rebirth.

The essence of "The Lake of Dreams" is illustrated by "a moment of perpetual surrender."[5] It is impossible to retreat to the temporary security of "The Sea of Crises"; it is equally impossible to dismiss the evil of "The Lake of Death." One must instead maintain a treacherous balance between the tension of the opposites and strive for the compensation of a new expectant largeness.[6]

In two interrelated poems, "The Hour of the Singer" and "When You Come Upon Him," the sacrifice of innocence which facilitates an expanded vision is rewarded by a stronger relationship with the Muse. The first poem depicts the subject in the apex of her life, "All you have sought you have already found." She is freed from "the years of false singing" and defined by "the blind mouth of the singer . . . in the naked pause between his words." In the final stanza, her vision is crystallized, the final secret behind her existence is illuminated:

> Now you comprehend your first and final lover
> in the dark receding planets of his eyes,
> and this is the hour when you know moreover
> that the god you have loved always
> will descend and lie with you in paradise. (*AM*, p. 60)

It is important to note here that the Muse-lover descends to the subject who has acquired, if only briefly, a moment of equality and reassurance.

In "When You Come Upon Him," the Muse is "the handsome two-horned one who waits / at the river of the world's end." The two-horned god is an allusion to the Celtic god Bran, lord of healing and of resurrection. The persona attests that she has served him well, "Tell him I bore the seed which was his dream, / tell him I made havoc in his name"; but the submission has been painful, the rewards few. Nevertheless, she has no intention of abandoning her journey. In the last stanza, despite a sense of weakness and dependency, she pleads only that her horizon be further enlarged:

> I was possessed and cold. I cried: *O shed*
> *the secret generations from your loins*
> *that these your ghostly children, Lord,*
> *shall lead me by the hair*
> *to the limits of the world.* (*AM*, p. 61)

The last line, reminiscent of the closing line in "It Comes Upon You" ("withdraw my fingers from your hair"), demonstrates the change in attitude, the maturity of submission, that the persona has achieved. Perhaps for this reason, her statements about poetry and about the inverse means of gathering knowledge in "Credo" can be accepted more easily:

> Believing everything, I do not expect
> you to believe an untenable myth
> or this incredible lie
> which is slowly turning you into truth. (*AM*, 59)

In the dissolution necessary to the destruction-creation process of alchemy, language, too, dissolves. The poems lie in "the naked pause" between words. The 'Word' can be communicated only through the flesh, the thesis of the poetry only through the flesh of dramatic situation.

At the conclusion of "The Lake of Dreams" MacEwen includes an ambitious nine-poem suite entitled "The Nine Arcana of the Kings." The first three poems appeared earlier in *A Breakfast for Barbarians*; and in the development of mood, and the choice of personae, the nine arcana closely resemble "The Papyrus of Meritaton" in *King of Egypt, King of Dreams*. But its inclusion in *The Armies of the Moon*, as Dragland points out, has a special function independent of its connection to earlier publications. Appearing at the end of the collection, it serves as a kind of functional ornament: the poetry itself is beautiful, but it is more impressive because "here the I of the other poems is exchanged for personae whose story gathers up and gives narrative substance to images and themes from the whole book."[7] Just as "The Papyrus of Meritaton" gave life to the theories of Atonism, the nine arcana dramatize "an acceptance of the essentially occasional and momentary nature of the breakthrough into peripheral space."[8] The nine poems form a cycle and establish a cosmos of their own in which the struggle with evil and myth central to the earlier sections is resolved.

In the first poem, "Arcanum One: The Prince," MacEwen recaptures the same mood of childlike wariness and joy which the lovers possess in *King of Egypt, King of Dreams*. The triangular relationship of king, brother, and sister is re-established with the exception that, even in the act of love, the presence of the king is inescapable:

> but in the evenings you wrote my name
> with a beetle and a moon, and lay upon me
> like a long broken necklace which had fallen
> from my throat, and the king loved you
> most in the morning, and his glamourous love
> lay lengthwise along us all the evening. (*AM*, p. 64)

In "Arcanum Two: The Conspirator," this mood of peaceful love is broken. The prince is caught between opposing forces—his sister and the king, the moon and the sun: "why do you sail like this between your sister / and the distant king?" The river which carries him away and brings him back, the "worried river," seems to represent an uncheckable flow of change and reality. The next poem, "Arcanum Three: The Death of the Prince," describes the violent assassination of the brother. The princess now broken and alone, despises the "crown" symbolic of her lover's destruction:

> He was destroyed upon the marble floor
> Between the fountain and the pillars
> And I bent over to call his name,
> His secret name whose syllables were thunder—
> Then I took the heavy crown and threw it in the river.
>
> (*AM*, p. 66)

The painful and eternal vigil of the female is the theme of the next three poems; until finally, in "Arcanum Seven: The Return," the prince rejoins her on "the bed of ebony and straw." But much has altered in the centuries of their separation—the brother comes "undead, unborn," a "Ghost of the morning." The interpretation of him as a reincarnation of Mercurius is supported first by the golden ring and crown he wears like the "glittering prison" in "Jewellery" and second by the fact that his soul is "a blazing ornament." The princess mourns that their honest love can never again be as simple as it once was: "the world will loathe our love of salt and fire / and none will let you call me sister here."

In the final poem, "Arcanum Nine: The Ring," "the living ghost of the king" haunts the lovers. His presence represents evil, the "awful sun" of the outside world, and reminds the prince that the innocence sacrificed in the struggle for an expanded vision can never be regained:

> and we are the end of his ancient line,
> your seed a river of arrested time
> whose currents bring the cursed crown
> forever back to the foot of this bed—
> the double crown of those who wear
> the kingdoms of heaven and hell on their head.
>
> (*AM*, p. 72)

The "cursed crown" is the reward of self-exploration: it is a symbol of power but also of terrifying responsibility.

The progressive development of MacEwen's use of her mythic source material culminates in "The Nine Arcana of the Kings." These poems represent the best of her poetry—their structure and substance reflecting through drama her fascination with the destruction-creation cycles of alchemy. Within their circular pattern, the nine poems narrate the story of the sister-brother lovers and their father the king, beginning with an innocent love, tracing the complications which eventually lead to death and separation, and ending with rebirth and a reunion that is all the richer for its combination of "heaven" and "hell." The connections between the prince and alchemy are frequent but never obtrusive: his body is alternatively "a living syllable / in his [the king's] golden script," "founting water," "a long broken necklace" or "Ghost of the morning." Similarly, the king is "the very lord of gold" whose shed blood is the "birth" of the prince's soul. In death, the prince is assailed by "silvery guards"; he comes to his lover as a reincarnated Muse figure, as Zeus in mythology came to Leda: "Your tired wings were songs among the leaves / and on my thighs you left your shining unreal seed." The once simple love between brother and sister grows in dimension until the circle is complete: the lovers in symbolic union wear, like the poet herself, the "cursed" double crown, emblem of the unity of opposites. Rich with the fullness of paradox and emotion, "The Nine Arcana" are called a gift by Dragland, the realization of the secrets of alchemy by Davey, and vibrant examples of poetry in which "the expository is obliterated," by Gustafson.[9]

The concluding poem in *The Armies of the Moon* is "Apollo Twelve"—a poem which reveals that the journey through "the breathless valley of the moon" has not ended but just begun. The trip through "inner" space, symbolized as a confrontation with the silver armies in the title poem, has been merely a preparation for passage into new galaxies. The astronaut becomes "the satellite of his own dream" while orbiting "the white world of his youth." As he progresses, his mental maturity leads him irresistibly towards an exploration of further mysteries: "Now up the weightless slopes of time he climbs / Through vacuous doorways to the gasping dark beyond." As a translator of the "gasping" dark, MacEwen writes poetically and dreamily, but with moments of startling clarity—moments which strive to lift us out of the narrow confines of our own horizons.

6

The Dancer: Noman

There, beyond the arch, is the forest. There is the naked, ancient door. You have only to pass under the arch to be free, to be away from this place, but you watch the arch and grow afraid, for the arch is watching you. The little King and the Fairy Queen are watching you. And all the trees are silently screaming.

This passage from "Kingsmere" best expresses the tension between invitation and warning which animates MacEwen's collection of short stories, *Noman*. Crossing through the archway, which is located in the historic 'ruins' of W.L. Mackenzie King's estate, promises the possibility of a future but demands the destruction of the past. Set within the realm of the safe and the familiar, the arch opens onto the unknown, onto a region where sentimentalized myth ("the little King and the Fairy Queen") is replaced by alarming and challenging realities. The contemplation of similar archways and the decision to cross through them, either consciously or unconsciously, is the uniting concern of each character and story of *Noman*.

Here, for almost the first time, MacEwen consistently uses a recognizable Canadian setting, drawing upon those familiar details of landscape and social expectation which lend drama and credibility to her themes. But it is evident as early as her dedication ("to all the strangers in Kanada") that her constant allegiance to living myth, paradox, and the union of the holy and obscene has not been forgotten. The accomplishment of *Noman*, like that of *King of Egypt, King of Dreams* and *The Armies of the Moon*, is to make the fantastic, but not incredible, private vision of the author accessible to the reader:

> The golden arrow becomes bow and arrow, the messiah becomes social iconoclast, and the horsemen ride right out of *Revelation* into a modern country carnival. The process of revitalization takes the symbolic figures of her stories out of allegory and the so-called Dark Ages into a modern baroque sensibility.[1]

In *Noman*, MacEwen integrates the magical and esoteric landscapes of Egypt, the Middle East, and Greece with that of Canada. "Kanada" is Noman's-land. It is here, as it was in *A Breakfast for Barbarians*, a world of bacon and eggs and of nonrevelation.[2] The result of the integration is possibility—the possibility of an individual, even a national identity, and the possibility, to use the words of Robertson Davies, of a knowledge "That the marvellous is indeed an aspect of the real."[3]

The structure of *Noman*, reflecting implicitly both the cyclical motion associated with the destructive-creative process in alchemy and the binary structure of reality, is central to the success of the collection. The final section, "Noman," is comprised of two short stories, each with the same set of characters but a different narrator; this section touches upon key ideas already introduced in the seven preceding stories. Characters reappear, images recur, and *Noman* achieves an overall effect of unity. Finally, by reflecting upon and illuminating events which occur in previous chapters and by adding the striking disclosure of its own revelations, the conclusion is, in many ways, the actual beginning. The beginning-ending paradox is a MacEwen trademark: the endings of her collections of poetry and short stories take the reader back to the beginnings of these collections and also forward to an anticipation of new material, new levels of meaning. The structural organization of MacEwen's collections which culminate in the beginning-ending paradox complements her concern to reveal the mythic in the mundane—in short, to demonstrate that the ordinary is extraordinary. Paradox and paradoxical situations can induce wonder and help the reader to awaken his mind, to view himself in a new and blinding light. Furthermore, the beginning-ending paradox and the embedded patterns of renewal so striking in MacEwen's writing seem to leave the reader expectant but never satisfied. This sense of anticipation, reappearing in the prose of *Noman*, comes closest to definition in "Animal Syllables" from *The Fire-Eaters*—a poem which, like MacEwen herself, "leaves no tracks":

Dark, I build a beachfire and thought about the flames and the earth. In the darkness I constructed a fire; in the midst of the fire I began to gather another darkness. (*FE*, p. 42)

In *Noman*, MacEwen offers no answers. In keeping with the dynamism of myth, she articulates only process, offers only endings which blossom into new beginnings.

Noman, the major character of the last two stories, becomes symbolic of all those characters who precede him. The Muse incarnate, a searching mystic fashioned after Julian and Akhenaton, he initiates paradoxical situations. He enacts the ritualistic primitivism of the dance, and, in dancing, he imitates the infinite turning of the circle and its enigmatic centre, "the / point of absolute inquiry." (*RF*, p. 49). Throughout, he "orchestrates the jokes and the tragedies";[4] he is

the hero of his author's apocalypse ... a life-spirit, Heraclitean fire, the divine imagination embodied in gods, demons and men, threatened always by extinction in this present world but always phoenix-like.[5]

Through her convincing portrayal of Noman, no *one* man, but Myth personified, MacEwen offers the reader the opportunity to begin his or her own journey—a chance to pass through the archway.

The quest begins with "House of the Whale," the story of a young Haida Indian, Lucas George, who leaves the security of his "myth drenched" reservation for the "moneyed" cities of Vancouver and Toronto. As in many of the stories, MacEwen uses a flashback technique: the character or characters, whose adventure, failure, or doom is already complete, bewilderingly reflect on the past for some clue to their future. In this instance, Lucas George, who is jailed and awaiting a trial for manslaughter, journeys back to his childhood in order to trace the events which led to his present situation. Superficially, he is writing to his strange friend Aaron who prophesied his failure; but in actuality he is searching himself for answers.

The focal point of "House of the Whale" is the fascination with myth and the differentiation between those myths which are outworn and those which have retained a sense of urgency and immediacy. George's childhood myths are colourful but harmless, like ghost stories whispered around a campfire. Always the legends and gods of his ancestors are externalized in some recognizable symbol, such as the decaying row of totems which "guard" the village, or the shaman with his pathetic magic of "dyed feathers and rattles." But despite the superstition and simplicity of his village, George maintains, perhaps unconsciously, a special reverence for his mythical heritage. His last memory of his grandfather is one in which the old man cleverly outwits those who would commercialize and cheapen the sacred tales of the Haida:

> Every researcher went away believing he alone had the authentic version of such and such a myth, straight from the Haida's mouth—but what none of them ever knew was that grandfather altered the tales with each re-telling. "It will give them something to fight about in their books"; he said. The older he got, the more he garbled the tales, shaking with wicked laughter in his big denim overalls when the little men with tape recorders and notebooks went away. (*N*, p. 8)

George's own defence of myth begins innocently, but it eventually erupts in violence. At a lumber camp in North Vancouver he tells "the guys in the bunkhouse" the tale of Gunarh, in which the wife of the god is deceived into consuming the sexual organs of her lover. The consumption of human flesh, particularly the genitals, which are essential for rebirth and regeneration, is closely related to the Christian tradition of holy communion in which the body of Christ, the saviour of life, is consumed. George's audience, however, perceives only crudity, and reduces his myth to a ribald joke:

> I never did finish the story, because they went on and on all night about what Gunarh's wife ate for breakfast, and Jake kept waking up and swearing he was never going to listen to one of my stories again, because it was for sure all Indians had pretty dirty minds to think up things like that. (*N*, p. 11)

In a similar confrontation between myth and reality the position is reversed; George recognizes immediately that the myth has been over-symbolized in art and divorced from any overtones of actuality:

> (the fine line, Aaron, between what is living and what is dead...what do I mean, exactly? That party you took me to once in that rich lady's house where everyone was admiring her latest artistic acquisition—a *genuine Haida* argillite sculpture. It illustrated the myth of Rhpisunt, the woman who slept with a bear and later on bore cubs, and became the Bear Mother. Well, there were Rhpisunt and the bear screwing away in black slate: Rhpisunt lay on her back, legs up, straddling the beast, her head thrown back and her jaws wide open with delight—and Mrs. What's-Her-Name kept babbling on and on about the 'symbolic' meaning of the carving until I got mad and butted in and told her it was

obviously a bear screwing a woman, nothing more, nothing less. She looked upset, and I was a little drunk and couldn't resist adding, 'You see, I too am *genuine Haida*!' And as the party wore on I kept looking back at the elaborate mantelpiece and the cool little slate sculpture, and it was dead, Aaron, it had *died*—do you see?) (*N*, pp. 7–8)

This passage recalls the wisdom of Ay in *King of Egypt, King of Dreams*:

If ever the weird stories of the creation and life of the universe could somehow be made real, they could destroy that universe; if ever a bull were to enter his mother and be reborn from her loins it would be an abomination. Thus the holy and the obscene exist side by side. (*KE,KD*, p. 235)

"Mrs. What's-Her-Name" has no notion of the "strange and dark" meanings behind myth. For her, the sculpture is "cool" rather than unsettling.

At this point in the story, George's awe for myth, his ability to distinguish between the fake and the genuine, is still a matter of heritage. As yet, the legends are external. However, when he meets Aaron, who takes him to Toronto, the situation begins to shift. Aaron tells George: "This, this is where you'll find your psyche"; he introduces George to the city by calling it "the House of the Whale" and then adds enigmatically, "I wish I could tell you that this city was just another myth, but it's not. It smacks too much of reality" (*N*, p. 14). Here then, when George is not consciously aware of his identity, when he drifts "on the sweet circumference of things looking into the centre," is where the myth begins to become internalized. George takes a job in construction as a "bucker" working on the high steel skeleton of a bank and begins to relive the tales of his past:

Amodeo offered me a hand when we first stepped out onto a beam, but I couldn't accept it, although the first minute up there was awful.... I kept telling myself that my people were the People of the Eagle, so I of all men should have no fear of walking where the eagles fly.... And when the first day was over I was awed to think I was still alive. The next day I imagined that the bank was a huge totem, or the strong man Aemaelk who holds the world up, and I started to like the work. (*N*, pp. 15–16)

Three years pass. The glory of George's childhood myths begins to tarnish, things begin to crumble around him "like the totems falling." Finally, in a seemingly unconscious and ritualistic act, he beats to death a man who, by calling George a "dirty Indian," challenges his heritage of relived myths.

MacEwen ends the story with a series of questions all of which confirm the fact that George is still enamoured of and blinded by his past. As a child he used to watch an argillite carver from Skidegate shape the figures of myth into stone, always imagining that there was "a little man, who lived inside the argillite and worked it from the inside out." George becomes in a sense "the little man" working myth from the inside out and sacrificing his own scrambled identity to the "countless figures" of legend:

> Have all the totems on my island fallen, or do some still stand?
> Will they stick my head up high on a cedar tree like they did to Gunarh?
> Will the Street of Walls fall down one day like the totems?
> What did you say I would find in the House of the Whale,
> Aaron? Aaron? Aaron? (*N*, p. 17)

The irony of George's fate lies in the fact that he is confined to prison and awaiting trial for defending something which he does not understand. To George, myth is divorced from reality; thus he remains on the circumference of the circle, never piercing to its core, in which, according to Jung and the Gnostics, the secrets of the self are embedded.

The next story, "Fire," dramatizes the hypnotic spell of myth. A young couple discovering such a rarity as a real fireplace in Toronto, are drawn into a re-enactment of primitive instinct and survival by the blaze of the flames. They celebrate their own private "potlache"—an ancient custom of burning private possessions to demonstrate one's freedom from the tyranny of materialism. The Indian custom of potlache is suggestive of the destructive potential of Boehme's fiery god and, also, of the destructive process in alchemy in which materials are broken down before being synthesized into a complex whole. At first, the characters' sacrifices to the fire are minor: a "five year old *Webster's* — (only 95 cents at Coles)," a greasy tea towel, and, ironically, a copy of *The Golden Bough* which burns with "intense heat." The fire exhilarates them, excites them to the point where the energy of the fire becomes a symbol of human survival:

> "Don't you have the strange feeling," he went on, untying his tie, "that it's freezing winter outside and we're living in a huge hostile forest, willing to sacrifice anything, our souls, even, to keep the fire going? (*N*, p. 23)

> "I wonder," said Chris, anxiously peering out of the window, "if we can hold out till morning," And his eyes had the quick, watchful, half-savage expression which the early settler must have worn as he gazed

out of his cabin on a winter night, looking for wolves, bears, Indians.
(*N*, p. 24)

The highlight of "Fire" is MacEwen's ability to make the couple's frenzy
believable. They become slaves to the fire. When, in the sobering light of
morning, the young woman views rationally the destruction, she is still
amazed. The spell of primitivism has not evaporated, the shadows of the
myth symbolized by the smoke and ashes, drift across her apartment:

> She stood there, in the smoky emptiness of the place, trying to remem-
> ber what had happened. She was thrust back to some point very distant
> in time. This, she thought, is what the caves of the early men look∂d
> like, full of strange chunks of carbon, white ash, charred stumps of
> nameless things that had once, perhaps, been trees, or bones. (*N*,
> p. 25)

MacEwen ends the story with the impression that the heroine, although
admitting that she has "gone off the deep end," has glimpsed something of
the compulsiveness of the renewal of myth.

The theme of uniting opposites in a single entity or symbol, achieved
most effectively in the character of Noman, is foreshadowed by "Snow," in
which a young Mediterranean named Grigori wishes to unite the heat of his
body with the dazzling cold of a 'Kanadian' winter. He regards the snow as a
symbol of divinity, creation, and unspoiled beauty:

> It was a kind of heavenly confetti, ambrosia or manna, and he rushed
> out half-mad at the first snowfall and lost himself in the sweet salt cold.
> He even dreamed of snow and he had a weird talent for predicting the
> next snowfall. He'd sleep and see tiny people coming down from the
> sky in parachutes that were snowflakes, a rain of infinitesimally small
> doves, ejaculations of white blossoms—the sperm of the great sleeping
> sky tree. (*N*, p. 76)

His companion, who finds no romance in a blizzard, tolerates but scarcely
understands his enthusiasm. She teaches him how to make snowstars and
snow angels, and together they 'paint' the fresh snowfalls as one would an
empty canvas. But for Grigori such superficial imprints upon the snow are
not sufficient to appease his desire for direct contact and ultimate union
with the mystery that the snow represents to him. Consequently, he sacrifices his own body in an effort to truly touch the unknown magic of the
snowfall:

she *was* surprised, though not totally, to find Grigori lying there at the bottom of the slide that gave off signals like the metal slab in *Space Odyssey*, with his Mediterranean hair all aflurry from the wind and his absolutely naked stone dead body wedged somehow into the snowdrift, and his arms outstretched at his sides as if he'd been making his last angel. (*N*, p. 80)

Grigori's wish throughout the story is to let "the cold feel *him*." Although he achieves his seemingly irrational goal he can only do so by first succumbing willingly to his own death. In many ways, the hero of "Snow" is like the Houdini and escape-artist heroes in *A Breakfast for Barbarians*: all are prisoners of the flesh. It is this ultimate bond, derived from the tradition of Christian mysticism, which prevents them from uniting totally with the spiritual.

With the exception of "Noman," the collection's most significant story is "Kingsmere," which appears exactly in the middle of the book. Its crucial positioning, preceded and followed by four stories, is no accident, for as mentioned earlier, it describes the uniting symbol of the archway. The first four stories, "House of the Whale," "Fire," "Day of Twelve Princes," and "The Oarsman and the Seamstress," respectively describe failure, altered awareness, tentative surrender, and desire. Together they represent an approach towards the archway, towards the unknown, and towards the elusive future. The last four stories, "The Second Coming of Julian the Magician," "Snow," and the two-part book of "Noman" follow a pattern of destruction, death, and rebirth which suggests the conditions of passing through the archway and the rewards which such an action yields. "Kingsmere" itself describes a disturbing discrepancy between the landscape as seen first, by day, and then, by night. Sunlit trivialities fade into the shadows of larger mysteries:

I mean that by night it's quite different. It's not a quaint picnic spot where one might drink tea and muse about the eccentric old gentleman who was once the Prime Minister of Kanada. You stroll across the black grass towards the gardens. The faint light from the tea-house kitchen allows you to make out the shimmering outlines of the arches and the walls. Behind them somewhere are trees, forest, vanished trails of Indians. (*N*, p. 53)

Finally, as one moves towards "the interior of the garden," the temporary vestiges of security crumble, exposing the vital dichotomies between past and future, between what is real and what is not:

Something isn't right. Into whose future are you moving?... You have spotted one very large arch at the far end of the field, and for a second you have an intense, blinding perception of the real nature of the place. This stone on stone, this reconstruction of a past that was never yours, this synthetic history. Only the furtive trees are real; they are the backdrop for an abandoned Greek theatre where the central paradoxes of man were once performed by actors wearing grotesque masks. The insane, incongruous pillars glimmer grey and pearlgrey in the halflight. Here there is a tension between past and future, a tension so real it's almost tangible; it lives in the stone, it crackles like electricity among the leaves. (*N*, p. 54)

Kingsmere looms in the imagination as a kind of "time-travel" place;[6] the archway or passage between the past and future, known and unknown. Similar to the Muse in his function as mirror in *The Shadow-Maker*, Kingsmere raises fundamental questions about human identity, questions which are, in turn, fundamental to the self-reflexive thrust of the fantastic in literature. In a joint review of MacEwen's work with that of Jacques Ferron and Gilles Vigneault, Kathy Mezei queries:

Are these peculiar images of frames, doors, and windows a coincidence or are the writers trying to suggest our passage from one world to another, trying to discover if our reality is real enough to be framed?[7]

On a less individual and more national level, Atwood suggests, Kingsmere invites an extrication from a superimposed past and movement towards a self-created future that will be more authentically Canadian:

Noman is the magician as Kanadian; his name, in addition to being Ulysses' pseudonym is probably intended to symbolize the famous Kanadian identity crisis.... With his thousand possible identities and his refusal to choose just one, he sets himself up (or is set up by his author) as Kanada incarnate. "Kanada," he sighs. "Paper-maker. Like a great blank sheet in the world's diary. Who'll make the first entry?"[8]

In Atwood's interpretation, it is Noman himself who makes the first entry, although what is written can only be guessed at. In any interpretation, the question "Into whose future are you moving" is perplexing. It is repeated on the final page of *Noman* when the magician returns, bringing the reader with him, for a final contemplation of the archway.

The story of "Noman" is comprised of two books, one narrated by Jubelas and the other by Kali. Each of these narrators, whose names are given to them by the hero, enjoys a strange relationship with the mysterious Noman who, in turn, is given his name by Kali on the first day they meet because he has *amne seeah*. Nicknaming and gameplaying with names become, in fact, minor fascinations throughout the story, but ultimately lead to the contemplation of larger mysteries. Like Kali, one begins with a small puzzle—"the meaning of Noman," the meaning of his name—and then moves outward only to be challenged by more significant meanings—"the meaning of Noman" becoming the enigma of his personality, his presence, and his ability to affect change—until finally, one confronts the meaning of one's self.

Like many of the preceding stories, "The Book of the Jubelas" is a flashback—a retelling of events which have already occurred. It begins with a description of the sudden and inexplicable death of Noman—a 'death' which is not solved until "The Book of Kali." Jubelas's concern is investigating this "crime" and, in attempting to do so, he recalls in detail the curious relationship which he and his wife shared with Noman.

His narrative is, at times, hilarious. The character of Jubelas seems to epitomize a dying breed of people who are enthusiastic about everything, astute about nothing, and irresistibly funny because they try so hard not to be. He begins by giving an account of their names, absolutely missing any of the underlying significance:

He [Noman] said we should have names that told something about what we were like. My name for instance—Jubelas—reminded him of Rome and jubilees and things like that. Well he was halfway right. I do have some Italian in my background, but also a lot of Irish and a spot of French-Kanadian. I'm not so sure about the name he gave my wife—Omphale—because I found out that it has some connection with belly-button. (*N*, p. 84)

The link between the narrator's character and his name is obvious enough. Omphale (shortened to the appropriately onomatopoeic Omph) is a mythological reference to Cybele, mother of gods. The couple is childless; but as their tie with the hero strengthens, Omphale dreams of having given "Miraculous birth to Noman in the middle of Bay Street after stars and planets had rolled around in her belly" (p. 97). Later, her first comment when she believes that Noman has died is "I miscarried him."

To say that Jubelas is baffled by Noman is an understatement. Convinced that Noman must be a foreigner, the narrator spends a great deal of his time saying "How Do You Do?" in "23 different languages" in the hope that he might unravel the mystery of Noman's past. He beautifully bungles this investigation but nevertheless uncovers one of the most essential characteristics of Noman:

(How can I describe him so you'll understand? First of all, he wasn't *bad*. He never lied, for instance—he just talked truth like it was a different kind. And he kind of pounced on you like a lion and ate you up...but very polite about it, very gentle. When he looked at you, his eyes were full of surprise, as if he never asked or expected to see the things he saw. Everything sort of played itself out before him. He himself *did* nothing, but he made it all happen.) (*N*, pp. 87–88)

The fact that Noman is both active and passive and, therefore, a figure who combines opposites, establishes him as a recognizable manifestation of Mac-Ewen's Muse. While he himself remains essentially unchanged, his influence causes a complete change in Jubelas.

The events which Jubelas recalls in an effort to understand his altered state of existence reveal Noman in his role as a mythical and mystic figure, and they bring into juxtaposition the marvellous and the mundane. First, the two friends meet a "bible-thumper" shouting "I am Alpha and Omega" on a Toronto street corner. Noman asks the man to explain and is abruptly discouraged:

"Are you questioning the word of God, my son?"

"No" (said Noman), "I just want to know what the word *is*."

"The word" (the guy went on), "is Alpha and Omega." Then he paused as if he just remembered something. "And I am Alpha and Omega."

"Well, I'm the whole alphabet," said Noman, leaning back against one of Eaton's plate–glass windows. "Will you let me stand beside you and say I am *Alpha and Omega*?"

"No. You are a charlatan, young man. Besides this is my corner."
(*N*, pp. 88–89)

The mystery of the Gnostic symbol of totality captured earlier in passages from *Julian the Magician* is, in its modern–day usage, completely obsolete, even farcical.

Next Jubelas and Noman call the phone numbers of various people to see if their names reflect either their personalities or life styles. Noman associates the names with romance and myth: Angelo Lucifori is imagined as the fallen angel Lucifer, John Incognito as an ex-spy. Jubelas, however, is much more practical and invariably right in his predictions: Lucifori owns "one leetle vegetable store," and Incognito runs an advertising agency. What is significant is that when the game is over, both men, especially Jubelas, feel disappointed. Even on the most trivial level, Noman has a knack for exposing fraudulence, and gradually Jubelas becomes disenchanted with his dull and predictable "Kanadian" environment.

Jubelas' change is rapid: he is forced to think (an unaccustomed act) and he becomes nervous and dissatisfied. In a scene which parodies an earlier act of aggression by Julian against the Machine in "The Second Coming of Julian the Magician," Jubelas totally destroys a jukebox. Finally, he begins to feel that he is losing his grip on Kanadian reality:

> Things started looking different to me...objects and buildings and people. Signs I'd never noticed before started screaming down at me from billboards. Mysterious things started happening in the subway. Noman couldn't explain it because, well, he was making it happen....
> "You're not going nuts, Jube, you're going sane; he said. "I know, it's hard to tell the difference." (*N*, p. 92)

Here Noman stresses the paradoxical idea that one must go insane to become sane. Later he says to Jubelas, "If Noman is hurting you then there's no-one hurting you after all....If Noman is blinding you, then you aren't blind" (p. 93). This statement is an allusion to Ulysses who, when captured by the Cyclops Polyphemus, gives his name as Noman. Thus when the monster, having been blinded by Ulysses, emerges from his cave crying "O friends, I die, and Noman gives the blow," his companions can only answer "If no man hurts thee it is the stroke of Jove, and thou must bear it." In MacEwen's story, the use of the word "no–one" also implies that Noman is "no man."

As Jubelas comes closer to the secret of Noman's identity, he discovers that his friend is a dancer; but the frenzy of the dance only frightens him:

> He kicked his heels down hard on the floor, and he danced, o man, did he dance! He laughed and sweated and his hair went flying all over his face, and I could see hordes of drunk Cossacks burning and looting villages. The little statues shook like they were scared; I was afraid when I stopped clapping they would all drop dead. And Noman was all muscle and nerve; he had all kinds of energy stored up, waiting. (*N*, p. 93)

The potential energy of Noman strengthens his significance as a Muse figure; his ritualistic dance becomes symbolic of both destruction and creation.

Jubelas' nervousness increasingly isolates him from society until finally, he indulges his impulses in an orgy of shoplifting. He confesses that he feels like "an animal, a savage in the city"; but Noman only smiles and replies that he himself is the savage. Unable to accept anything but a romantic or "foreign" view of Noman, Jubelas fails to understand the wisdom of paradox. It is perhaps for this reason that Noman plans the "Saturnal," the scene for his staged death. In mythology, the feast of Saturnalia was celebrated every year in the winter season in honour of the beneficent reign of Saturn which was known as the Golden Age. It was a holiday of unlicensed revellry and equality. In MacEwen's version, Noman 'dies' during the mock ceremony, thereby freeing himself from Jubelas, and freeing Jubelas from the last structures of false reality. Here the juxtaposition between myth and modern-day reality is extremely effective. The grandeur of the ancient Saturnalia is reduced to a gathering of four people with bread and homemade wine under a viaduct in the middle of Toronto, beneath the "sick-looking" and "jaundice yellow" planet Saturn. Even the death of Noman, as we learn later from Kali, is feigned. But the re-enactment of the myth is far more compelling than the logic of the situation: Jubelas is convinced of his own 'insanity' and his education is complete. Furthermore, Noman is linked with Saturn, the alchemical god of devouring who in Greek and Roman mythology eats his own children. Under the spell of a potion administered by the goddess Metis (Prudence), Saturn later disgorged his children in an act which is akin to Noman's active and passive release of Jubelas and Omphale.

MacEwen ends the story on a note of hope by circling back to the symbolic archway at Kingsmere. Jubelas, duped yet incurably optimistic, has now become the alien: "I feel like a foreigner who doesn't speak the right language. Or maybe everyone else is speaking the wrong language. '*Hace frio ¿ no es verdad?*'" (p. 101). His "investigations" are perhaps closer to the truth than ever before:

> maybe you'll tell me that you played a fool trick and aren't dead at all...? Wow, we'll laugh at that, and drunk as lords we'll sing and stagger all over the fields full of bees, the green fields, under the yellow laughter of the sun, over the rivers and streams and through the big arch that leads into the forest. (*N*, p. 102)

Although still unaware of exactly how he was changed, Jubelas is at least able to stand on the threshold of the arch.

In "The Book of Kali," MacEwen is much more explicit in her efforts to establish Noman as the genuine Muse who subsumes opposites and links the ordinary with the arcane. His story actually begins with an earlier selection from *Noman* entitled "Day of Twelve Princes" in which he is described as the child Samuel. Even as a young boy amid a bleak and poverty-ridden environment he hungers for myth and spiritualism. Samuel (whose name translates from the Hebrew as "god") is associated with dreams, energy, fire and earth. A sunlit bough outside his window is transformed imaginatively into a weapon of power:

And the sun ran its fingers along the body of the branch, tracing, exploring, transforming it into a warrior's golden bow, a weapon of pure fire, unstrung, divorced from the tree. And Samuel thought: Therefore this fire is also mine and the power that goes with it. (*N*, p. 26)

The strong connections which MacEwen has established between fire and divinity, between the fire that consumes and the fire that forges, give Noman, even as a child, the characteristics of the Muse.

Isolated from other children, Samuel imagines himself to be a young warrior surrounded by twelve princes, just as the Biblical Samuel, surrounded by the twelve tribes of Israel, was a great leader against the Philistine oppressors. His constant companion, the image of his spirit-father, rides to him from the realm of myth:

Samuel saw him often in his mind's eye—lord of princes. He smiled and a hundred suns rose and set, he rode snowy stallions forever through the deserts of his dreams and carried a long javelin set with a hundred precious stones. He wore large rings on his fingers, his voice was deep and clear, his hand calmed turbulent horses. (*N*, p. 31)

Samuel's real father, the weak and ineffectual Aubrey, seems to be an unfortunate intrusion of reality.

Already identified with the energy of fire, Samuel welcomes further communion with other elements, with powers greater than his own. He steals an Arabian horse from a visiting circus and finds in its speed and beauty an exhilarating freedom:

Samuel buried his face in Arab's mane and he knew himself to be a part of the beast; he was a centaur, and everything from his chest down was pure horse....The Arab knew his darkest thought, the Arab was an arrow shot from his desire, seeking its target....They rested in a field, and the Arab's wet head curved down like some great terrible swan to taste the grass. Samuel lay on the thick turf and laughed. "I am the earth, the turf, the trees, the fibres of fire in the Arab's body." (*N*, p. 37)

Here Samuel embraces the earth, the basic *prima materia* of alchemy. He identifies himself as a centaur, the mythological creature that was half-horse, half-man, which later became the zodiac symbol for Sagittarius, one of the fire signs in astrology.

Near the end of the story, Samuel and his mother Hannah move to the city where poverty and gang violence are imprinted upon the imagination of

the boy. He earns his place in the city by enduring a beating in an alley
during which his entourage of twelve princes undergoes a subtle change:

> And as he stumbled along toward Howland Street, second to the left, he
> heard a sound of laughter in the alleyway—wild laughter, sharp laugh-
> ter, the laughter of children, the kind you hear at carnivals. And when
> he turned around he saw twelve princes, one for every hour of the day,
> and their golden bows lay on the ground before them, and they held
> twelve white flags of surrender to the sun. (*N*, p. 46)

The terms of surrender are somewhat ambiguous: either Samuel yields up
his imaginary protectorate to the demands of reality or the princes themselves surrender to their master's instincts for survival. At any rate, Samuel
leaves them behind with his childhood.

It is Kali who rediscovers the mature Samuel, Noman. Her first impression establishes him as a destroyer, again associated with fire:

> I came to be standing downtown one day in late summer watching
> Noman demolish an old bank. Not *alone*, of course, he was with a crew
> of men employed by the Apocalyptic Demolition Co., and they were
> attacking one wall, pulling out cables and wires viciously, smashing
> away at the bricks. Noman was dressed in white, like an avenging angel,
> and as I watched, he bent over a red joint in the metal framework of the
> wall and attacked it with a torch. Loud flames issued from his fingers.
> (*N*, p. 104)

MacEwen uses rather obvious tactics to stress the connection between
Noman and the divine—the name chosen for Noman's employers, "the
Apocalyptic Demolition Co.," is deliberately blatant.

As Kali begins her relationship with Noman, the mythological references
and allusions become increasingly significant. The name chosen for her by
Noman is that of the wife of the dancing Siva in Hindu mythology; and, later
in the story, when Noman dances against the incongruous backdrop of
Toronto's industrialized skyline, she sees him as Siva, the creative destroyer:

> We approached a big skyway that was under construction....It was a
> kind of Stonehenge, an incomplete temple.
>   And then—
> he stepped quickly out of the car and threw off his coat, his shirt, his
> socks, his shoes, and laid them in a heap at the bottom of the cold pillar.
> It was full moon, a November night. Then he began to dance. Around
> and around, in and out between the pillars, the cranes, the small trucks

and pieces of machinery that had been left standing for the night. It was as if everything had been arranged for him, for his dance.

Siva, I thought, as I sat in the whirring silence of my car. (*N*, p. 111)

The modern industrial landscape becomes a temple, and Noman becomes the saint or dervish whose dance is a form of primitive and magical worship.

Throughout the story Noman is many things: he himself admits, "Kali, I am so many people." Kali discovers that he is Kanadian; she sees him as the alchemical god Mercurius with drops of water "falling from his arms and thighs like mercury" (p. 105); and, during their lovemaking, she makes bites like "the sign of the holy Fish," a traditional symbol of Christ, down the length of his body. At one point, she states "Noman *became* whatever he encountered" (p. 107); and finally, she interprets his dancing body as the word-thing metaphor used by MacEwen in earlier poems from *A Breakfast for Barbarians*:

> His back, from the shoulder-blades to the bottom of his spine, was the tightly stretched, triangular frame of a kite. I imagined that the organs in his body floated in a kind of fluid tension, a suspended flight. And as he danced and flew, his body broke into alphabets. (*N*, p. 111)

The phrases "fluid tension" and "suspended flight" strengthen Noman's association with the alchemical god Mercurius.

Noman's potential for destruction, already demonstrated in his influence over Jubelas and Omphale, is emphasized throughout Kali's narrative. In order to settle a dispute with Kali about his past, he smashes a statuette of a Canaanite goddess against his apartment wall; his apartment itself is "a kind of Eden" primeval and forbidding. Here the lovers share their own frenzied potlache, and their lovemaking is described as a strange combination of annihilation and release:

> We emerged from the night beaten and bruised, as if we'd come out of a den of lions, or had become gladiators, bloody and victorious after the game. My loins were broken; armies had marched over them and crushed them into sand. (*N*, p. 114)

> We dove into each other, each speaking his own separate savage tongue. When I kissed him I whispered, *This* is for the blind who love with their mouths and hands....
>
> And our limbs, changing, moving, wrote out new alphabets in the darkness, formed new constellations. We smelled of salt, and fire and flowers. (*N*, p. 113)

The sexual union of Noman and Kali is analogous to the process of alchemy: it begins with destruction and ends with the formation of new harmonies. Through suffering, the lovers gain new possibilities—the sharing of "fire" and "flowers."

When Noman reveals his past to Kali, he becomes more amorphous rather than more concrete. Once he was a clown in a circus, who each night removed his make-up in a private ritual; the make-up becomes layers of masks similar to those of the Muse in two earlier poems, "The Return" and "The Golden Hunger." At another time, he describes himself as the "Houdini" Muse struggling with the boundaries of his own flesh. Once with Kali, his mirror image is reflected "a million times smaller and smaller into a microcosm" (p. 109). Finally, after the celebration of his dance, Kali remarks, "He had turned into a kind of vapour, a mist that I could have sprayed on my hair" (p. 112).

The final release of Noman from the mundane and predictable world, as represented by the shallow Jubelas and the maternal Omphale, is prompted by Kali: she decides that he must "die" and, in so doing, become "re-born." Thus the bloody sacrifice of the "Saturnal" is staged for the onlookers, and Noman escapes to the realm of new possibilities. Not surprisingly, MacEwen places Noman's future in the midst of Kingsmere. He and Kali return to the ruins at night, when the fraudulent pillars and statues of a borrowed history are distorted by moonlight and mist. Noman immediately finds the arch, "like an ancient door that led into the forest, the final mystery," and moves towards it irresistibly:

> "Coming Kali?" he asked again, and when I didn't answer he went on farther into the spooky greyness nearer and nearer the arch. I half rose to follow him, but just then a sudden flash of lightning lit up the field and froze the terrible door in a violent relief.
> "Noman, what are we *doing* here?" I cried. 'whose past have we stolen? Into whose future are we moving?"
> And he (swiftly removing his clothes) called back to me—"Why, our own, of course!"
> And blithely stepped, stark naked, through the arch. (*N*, p. 120)

Noman, as the divine Muse, is the first to pass through the archway; the first to destroy a cloying existence and embrace the authenticity of the forest. In so doing, he calls for Kali and for all those who are courageous enough to follow him.

The idea of Noman's future is so tantalizing that one finishes the book with a feeling that the beginning has just been reached. It is difficult, in fact impossible, not to see Noman in retrospect; almost every story shifts slightly in meaning under the influence of the major character and the consequence of his passage through the arch. Frank Davey sums up the achievement of Noman as Siva in the following:

> Siva encompasses many of the characters and events of the other stories in the collection. In his consuming "fire" aspect he is the god of the story by that name. His is the Mediterranean heat which tries disastrously in "Snow" to unite with the Canadian winter. His role in disdaining the present commercial reality of Toronto repeats in part the plot of "House of Whale." As Siva, Noman subsumes the Haida myth's Gunarh, finding not only his "psyche" but the future which Lucas George is denied. Siva also encompasses the heroes of MacEwen's novels. In joining himself with Kali/Parvati/Shakti he combines fire and love in the same way that Julian's Christ does in combining the Holy Ghost and the Virgin Mary; in passing through Kingsmere's ruins in order to approach new possibility, he accomplishes a union of the obscene and the holy similar to that recommended by It Neter Ay, MacEwen's spokesman in *King of Egypt, King of Dreams.*[9]

Noman, fulfills MacEwen's intention to create myth, to animate myth by blending rather than divorcing it from reality. Yet *Noman* also beckons to the reader, calling on him to cross through the archway, leaving him to wonder what is on the other side. When MacEwen publishes again the reader might expect to find not a mirror of the fantastic, but an extension of his own "Kanadian" reality. The discovery of one is the realization of the other.

Notes

NOTES TO THE PREFACE

1. Merle Shain, "Some of Our Best Poets are Women," *Maclean's Magazine* (March 1973), pp. 106–7.
2. Gwendolyn MacEwen, *The Armies of the Moon* (Toronto: Macmillan, 1972), p. 75.
3. Frank Davey, "Gwendolyn MacEwen: The Secret of Alchemy," *Open Letter* (second series), 4 (Spring 1973), p. 12.
4. Based on personal interview with MacEwen, 15 May 1974.

NOTES TO CHAPTER ONE

1. Interview with Gwendolyn MacEwen, 1 May 1979.
2. *15 Canadian Poets*, ed. Gary Geddes and Phyllis Bruce (Toronto, 1970), p. 280.
3. Interview
4. Interview
5. Interview
6. *15 Canadian Poets*, p. 280.
7. *Six Theosophic Points* (Ann Arbor, 1958), p. 6.
8. "A Tour de Force," *Evidence* 8 (1964), p. 140.
9. (Edmonton, 1970), p. 174.
10. *15 Canadian Poets*, p. 280.
11. "A Complex Music," *Canadian Literature* 21 (Summer 1964), p. 70.
12. Bowering, p. 71.
13. *University of Toronto Quarterly* 42 (1972), p. 372.
14. "Figments of a Northern Mind," *Tamarack Review* 31 (Spring 1964), p. 91.
15. *Open Letter* (second series) 4, Spring 1973, pp. 17–19.
16. *University of Toronto Quarterly* 31 (1961), p. 448.
17. "Seedtime in a Dark May," *Alphabet* 4 (June 1962), p. 70.
18. *Quarry* 22:2 (Spring 1973), p. 71.
19. *Quarry* 19:2 (Winter 1970), pp. 57–58.
20. p. 59.
21. "The Canadian Poetry Underground," *Canadian Literature* 13 (Summer 1962), p. 66.
22. "Seedtime," p. 70.
23. Wilson, p. 448.
24. Fox, p. 57.
25. "Circumventing Dragons," *Canadian Literature* 55 (Winter 1973), p. 107.
26. *The Fiddlehead* 94 (Summer 1972), p. 119.
27. Interview
28. *Rhymes and Reasons*, ed. John Robert Colombo (Toronto, 1971), p. 64.
29. "MacEwen's Muse," *Canadian Literature* 45 (Summer 1970), p. 31.
30. *Secrets*, p. 9.
31. *Secrets*, p. 23.
32. *Secrets*, p. 12.
33. *Canadian Literature* 71 (Winter 1976), p. 22.
34. Warwick, p. 24.
35. Warwick, p. 34.
36. "Language of our Time," *Canadian Literature* 29 (Summer 1966), p. 67.
37. *From There to Here* (Erin, Ont., 1974), p. 22.
38. "To Improvise an Eden," *Edge* 2 (Spring 1964), p. 121.
39. *15 Canadian Poets*, p. 280.
40. *Essays on Canadian Writing* 1 (Winter 1974), p. 21.
41. *The Canadian Imagination*, ed. David Staines (Cambridge, Mass., 1977), p. 100.
42. *Butterfly on Rock* (Toronto, 1970), pp. 181–182.

NOTES TO CHAPTER TWO

1. Margaret Atwood, "MacEwen's Muse," *Canadian Literature* 45 (Summer 1970), p. 25.
2. Eds. H. Read, M. Fordham, G. Adler, trans. R.F.C. Hull, 2nd ed., Bolligen Series XX, vol. 12 (Princeton, 1968), p. 270.
3. Jung, p. 257.
4. Jung, p. 243.
5. Jacob Boehme, *Six Theosophic Points* (Ann Arbor, 1958), p. 6.
6. "They Shall Have Arcana," *Canadian Literature* 21 (Summer 1964), p. 42.
7. Boehme, p. 6.
8. "Arcana," p. 42.

9. As quoted by Frank Davey, "Gwendolyn MacEwen: The Secret of Alchemy," *Open Letter* (second series) 4 (Spring 1973), pp. 6–7.
10. As quoted by R.M. Grant, *Gnosticism and Early Christianity* (New York, 1966), p. 12.
11. Atwood, p. 27.
12. Christopher Ringrose, "Vision Enveloped in Night," *Canadian Literature* 53 (Summer 1972), p. 103.
13. Elizabeth Waterston, "Akhenaton in Art," *Journal of Canadian Fiction* 1:3 (Summer 1972), p. 76.
14. Waterston, p. 76.

NOTES TO CHAPTER THREE

1. Frank Davey uses this phrase in *From There to Here* (Erin: Press Porcepic, 1974), p. 178: "Throughout, the poetry assumes the binary structure of reality— at its highest level the celestial versus the terrestrial, at lower levels the sun versus the moon, light versus dark, man versus woman, sanity versus madness." The word "binary" is used by Davey in "Gwendolyn MacEwen: the Secret of Alchemy," *Open Letter* (second series) 4 (Spring 1973), p. 13: "Repeatedly the poetry tells us that the mythic structure of reality is binary.... Every part of creation has its other." Davey's use of the term "binary," like my own in the present study, does not depart from the dualistic philosophy of the Neoplatonic and hermetic traditions.

2. As quoted by David Daiches, *Critical Approaches to Literature* (New York, 1956), p. 162.
3. Jacob Boehme, *Six Theosophic Points* (Ann Arbor, 1958), p. 6.
4. D.G. Jones, "Language of Our Time," *Canadian Literature* 29 (Summer 1966), p. 67.
5. *The Confessions of Jacob Boehme*, ed. W. Scott Palmer, with an introduction by Evelyn Underhill (New York, 1920), p. 26.
6. D.G. Jones, p. 67.
7. Peter Revell, "Images," *Alphabet* 13 (June 1967), p. 96.
8. "Gwendolyn MacEwen: The Secret of Alchemy," *Open Letter* (second series) 4 (Spring 1973), pp. 13–14.

NOTES TO CHAPTER FOUR

1. Ed. H. Read, M. Fordham, G. Adler, trans. R.F.C. Hull, 2nd ed., Bolligen Series XX, vol. 5 (Princeton, 1968), pp. 337–38.
2. *The Confessions of Jacob Boehme*, ed. W. Scott Palmer, with an introduction by Evelyn Underhill (New York, 1920), p. xxviii.
3. Jung, p. 24.

4. As quoted by Eric S. Rabkin in *The Fantastic in Literature* (Princeton, 1976), p. 222.
5. p. 222.
6. *Open Letter* (second series) 4 (Spring 1973), p. 15.
7. Jung, p. 12.
8. Jung, p. 12.

NOTES TO CHAPTER FIVE

1. *Quarry* 21:4 (Autumn 1972), p. 57.
2. p. 59.
3. "Gwendolyn MacEwen: The Secret of Alchemy," *Open Letter* (second series) 4 (Spring 1973), p. 23.
4. "Secrets," p. 22.
5. "McGill Park, Summer," *AM*, p. 55.
6. Dragland, p. 61.
7. Dragland, p. 61.
8. Dragland, p. 61.
9. "Circumventing Dragons," *Canadian Literature* 55 (Winter 1973), p. 108.

NOTES TO CHAPTER SIX

1. Linda Rogers, "Distorting Mirror," *Canadian Literature* 58 (Autumn 1973), p. 110.
2. Margaret Atwood, "Canadian Monsters," *The Canadian Imagination*, ed. David Staines (Cambridge, Mass., 1977), p. 110.
3. *Fifth Business* (Markham, Ont., 1977), p. 199.
4. Rogers, p. 111.
5. Robert Gibbs, "Review of *Noman*," *Journal of Canadian Fiction* 2:1 (Winter 1973), p. 93.
6. Atwood, p. 111.
7. *Quarry* 22:2 (Spring 1973), p. 71.
8. Atwood, p. 112.
9. "Gwendolyn MacEwen: The Secret of Alchemy," *Open Letter* (second series) 4 (Spring 1973), p. 12.

Bibliography

PRIMARY SOURCES

Poetry
Selah and *The Drunken Clock:* (privately-printed, 1961) OP
The Rising Fire: Contact Press, Toronto, 1963 OP
A Breakfast for Barbarians: Ryerson Press, Toronto, 1966 OP
The Shadow-Maker: MacMillan of Canada, Toronto, 1969 OP
The Armies of the Moon: MacMillan, Toronto, 1972 OP
Magic Animals: (Selected Poems) MacMillan, Toronto, 1975
The Fire-Eaters: Oberon Press, Ottawa, 1976
Trojan Women: Exile Editions, Toronto, 1981
The T.E. Lawrence Poems: Mosaic Press, Oakville, 1982
Earthlight: (Selected Poems) 1963–1982; General Publishing, Toronto, 1982

Novels
Julian the Magician: MacMillan, Toronto, and Corinth Books, N.Y. 1963/OP
King of Egypt, King of Dreams: MacMillan, Toronto, 1971 OP

Short Stories
Noman: Oberon Press, Ottawa, 1972

Travel
Mermaids and Ikons: A Greek Summer: Anansi, Toronto, 1978

Juvenile
The Chocolate Moose: N/C Press, Toronto, 1979
The Honey Drum: Mosaic Press, Oakville, 1983

Theatre
The Trojan Women: a new version. St. Lawrence Centre, November/December 1978

LP Recordings and Tapes
Gwendolyn MacEwen: High Barnet Co. (cassette); *Canadian Poets 1:* CBC, 1966 (LP); *Open Secrets:* CBC, 1972 (LP); *Canadian Poets on tape:* OISE (tape/cassette)

SECONDARY SOURCES

Books
Boehme, Jacob. *The Confessions of Jacob Boehme*. Ed. W. Scott Palmer, with an introduction by Evelyn Underhill, New York: Knopf, 1920.
———. *Six Theosophic Points*. Ann Arbor: University of Michigan Press, 1958.
Colombo, John Robert, ed. *How Do I Love Thee*. Edmonton: Hurtig, 1970.
———. *Rhymes and Reasons: Nine Canadian Poets Discuss Their Work*. Toronto: Holt Rinehart and Winston, 1971.
Daiches, David. *Critical Approaches to Literature*. New York: Norton, 1956.

Davey, Frank. *From There To Here*. Erin, Ont.: Press Porcepic, 1974.

Davies, Robertson. *Fifth Business*. Markham, Ont.: Penguin, 1977.

Geddes, Gary, and Phyllis Bruce, ed. *15 Canadian Poets*. Toronto: Oxford University Press, 1970.

Grant, R.M. *Gnosticism and Early Christianity*. New York: Columbia University Press, 1966.

Jones, D.G. *Butterfly on Rock*. Toronto: University of Toronto Press, 1970.

Jung, C.G. *Psychology and Alchemy*. Ed. H. Read, M. Fordham, G. Adler, trans. R.F.C. Hull, 2d ed., Bolligen Series XX, vol. 12. Princeton: Princeton University Press, 1968.

_____. *Symbols of Transformation*. Ed. H. Read, M. Fordham, G. Adler, trans. R.F.C. Hull, 2d ed., Bolligen Series XX, vol. 5. Princeton: Princeton University Press, 1968.

Rabkin, Eric S. *The Fantastic in Literature*. Princeton: Princeton University Press, 1976.

Articles

Atwood, Margaret. "Canadian Monsters," *The Canadian Imagination*. Ed. David Staines. Cambridge, Mass.: Harvard University Press, 1977, pp. 97–122.

_____. "MacEwen's Muse," *Canadian Literature* 45: 23–32.

Davey, Frank. "Gwendolyn MacEwen: The Secret of Alchemy," *Open Letter* (second series) 4, Spring 1973: 5–23.

Gose, E.B. "They Shall Have Arcana," *Canadian Literature* 21: 36–45.

Slonim, Leon. "Exoticism in Modern Canadian Poetry," *Essays on Canadian Writing* 1: 21–26.

Warwick, Ellen D. "To Seek A Single Symmetry," *Canadian Literature* 71: 21–34.

Reviews

Barrett, Elizabeth. "A Tour de Force," *Evidence* 8 (1964): 140–43.

Bartley, Jan. "Into the Fire," *Open Letter* (3d series) 5: 85–87.

Bowering, George. "The Canadian Poetry Underground," *Canadian Literature* 13: 66–67.

_____. "A Complex Music," *Canadian Literature* 21: 70–71.

Dragland, Stan. Review of *The Armies of the Moon*, *Quarry* 21:4: 57–62.

Fox, Gail. Review of *The Shadow-Maker*, *Quarry* 19:2: 57–59.

Gibbs, Robert. "Review of *Noman*," *Journal of Canadian Fiction* 2:1: 93.

Godfrey, Dave. "Figments of a Northern Mind," *Tamarack Review* 31: 90–91.

Gustafson, Ralph. "Circumventing Dragons," *Canadian Literature* 55: 105–8.

Hornyansky, Michael. "Review of *The Armies of the Moon*," *University of Toronto Quarterly* 42: 366–80.

Jones, D.G. "Language of our Time," *Canadian Literature* 29: 67–69.

Mandel, Eli. "Seedtime in a Dark May," *Alphabet* 4: 70.

Mezei, Kathy. Review of *Noman*, *Quarry* 22:2: 70–71.

Revell, Peter. "Images," *Alphabet* 13: 96–97.

Ringrose, Christopher. "Vision Enveloped in Night," *Canadian Literature* 53: 102–4.

Rogers, Linda. "Distorting Mirror," *Canadian Literature* 58: 110–11.

Sherman, Joseph. "Review of *The Armies of the Moon*," *The Fiddlehead* 94: 118–20.

Sowton, Ian. "To Improvise an Eden," *Edge* 2: 119–24.

Waterston, Elizabeth. "Akhenaton in Art," *Journal of Canadian Fiction* 1:3: 76–77.

Wilson, Milton. "Letters in Canada 1961: Poetry," *University of Toronto Quarterly* 31: 448.

Gwendolyn MacEwen: Born 1941, Toronto, Canada. Her work has appeared in most Canadian literary publications and is represented in most Canadian anthologies. Her writings include poetry, fiction, drama for radio and theatre, juvenile fiction and a travel book. She has travelled in Israel, Egypt and Greece, and has done translations from the contemporary Greek poet, Yannis Ritsos. She is currently living in Toronto, and working on a new novel and a new stage play.

She is the winner of the Governor General's Award for *The Shadow-Maker*, 1970; the A.J.M. Smith Poetry Award for *The Armies of the Moon*, 1973.

Index